MEANING AND TRUTH
IN
WITTGENSTEIN'S *TRACTATUS*

JANUA LINGUARUM

STUDIA MEMORIAE
NICOLAI VAN WIJK DEDICATA

edenda curat

C. H. VAN SCHOONEVELD

INDIANA UNIVERSITY

SERIES MINOR

NR. LXIV

1968

MOUTON

THE HAGUE · PARIS

MEANING AND TRUTH IN WITTGENSTEIN'S *TRACTATUS*

by

JAMES C. MORRISON
UNIVERSITY OF TORONTO

1968
MOUTON
THE HAGUE · PARIS

LIBRARY OF CONGRESS CATALOG CARD NUMBER: 68-15536

Printed in The Netherlands by Mouton & Co., Printers, The Hague.

To my mother

and father

Es ist viel leichter, in dem Werk eines grossen Geistes die Fehler und Irrtümer nachzuweisen, als von dem Werth desselben eine deutliche und vollständige Entwicklung zu geben.

Schopenhauer

PREFACE

Wittgenstein's *Tractatus*, like many important philosophical works, is not easy to understand. But the usual difficulties arising from the subject matter are enhanced by the way in which it is written. The extremely condensed and aphoristic style which Wittgenstein employs poses great problems of interpretation — indeed necessitates interpretation — and makes greater demands upon the reader, than a book written in a more conventional, straightforward style. In the latter case, the writer has to some extent done the reader's thinking for him by setting down explicitly his thoughts and their relationships. Everything has been placed in full view, as it were, and the reader has merely to comprehend it. His relation to the writer, at least in the beginning, is passive — he is a listener. But when confronted with the terseness of the *Tractatus* the reader must assume from the start a more active role, for what makes up a given idea or thought, the structure and relationships of the parts of the argument to one another and to the whole, are not always immediately apparent. Much is latent and implicit, and it becomes the task of the reader to enter into the idea and bring it fully to light within his own understanding. This is not always easy, particularly because one can never be *sure* that what one understands is what the writer intended to say. But if it cannot be successfully accomplished, at least to some extent, everything will remain incomprehensible, strange, and paradoxical. This is why, I think, Wittgenstein says in his Preface:

> Perhaps this book will be understood only by someone who has himself already had the thoughts expressed in it — or at least similar thoughts. — So it is not a textbook. —[1]

[1] Ludwig Wittgenstein, *Tractatus Logico-Philosophicus*, trans. by D. F. Pears and B. F. McGuinness (London, Routledge & Kegan Paul, 1961), p. 3.

In light of the above remarks I will state the purpose of this book as an attempt to "uncover" and make explicit some of these fundamental thoughts. My discussion focuses upon two of the central problems of the *Tractatus*, meaning and truth, and aims at giving a coherent and systematic statement of Wittgenstein's views on these, and related problems. My approach is basically expository, in that I try to reconstruct Wittgenstein's thought, in regard both to its content and also the general structure of the argument. (Thus, I have restricted my own criticisms to the final pages of the Conclusion.) Supplementary to my expository task I criticize what I believe to be some of the more important misinterpretations and erroneous critisisms of the *Tractatus*, specifically in regard to problems in the theory of meaning . My main reason for undertaking such criticism is not merely to show where others are wrong, but rather to elucidate what the *Tractatus* itself means. Also, I wish to call attention to, and emphasize, certain elements of Wittgenstein's thought which tend to be unduly neglected or ignored. Among these I believe the most important are the doctrines of logical form, showing (*zeigen*) and mysticism, which are treated primarily in Chapter IV.

What I say is thus an *interpretation*, not a mere paraphrase of the text. However, although I hope that what I say is an accurate reflection of the real import of the doctrines discussed, I do not claim that it is *the* authoritative and final account of those doctrines. At most I hope that what I have presented is coherent and plausible, and that it may prove illuminating, even where it has gone astray. Needless to say, I have not attempted to discuss everything, but I believe that what I have chosen is central to the content and significance of the *Tractatus* as a whole. However one may understand the details of the views of the *Tractatus*, and its general philosophical implications, I think one must agree that the theory of meaning lies at its basis. This is the element around which all else is focused. Furthermore, once the theory of meaning has been fully developed the theory of truth and falsehood follows quite naturally from it. In addition, although I have not discussed in detail *all* the writings of other philosophers dealing with the *Tractatus* and the problems raised in it (nor have I intended to do so) I have tried to take many of them into account, emphasizing that which I feel to be most relevant and important for my own purposes.[2] Finally, I have made use of two other philosophical works by Wittgenstein from the same period, namely, the *Notebooks 1914-1916* and the short essay, "Some Remarks on Logical Form." I have used them primarily for the purposes of illustration and emphasis, not as a basis for my own interpretation of the *Tractatus* itself. To use them as bases for interpretation would not have been justifiable for the simple reason that one can never assume that a philosopher does not change his mind and say something in one work which is not wholly consistent with what he says in another.

I have made use of both English translations of the *Tractatus*, that of Ogden, which first appeared in 1922, and that of Pears and McGuinness, recently published in 1961. All direct quotations, however, have been taken from the latter's version. Moreover, I have consistently followed their phrasings in my own text, especially in regard to technical terminology. The main advantage of the Pears and McGuinness version seems to lie in its more consistent renderings of technical terms, and the attempt to express a different German word by a different English one. However, wherever questions of terminology seemed crucial I included the German word or phrase in brackets next to the English.

This book is divided into three main parts. The first part (Chapter I) sketches some of the basic ideas embodied in Wittgenstein's ontology. The second part (Chapters II, III, and IV) deals with Wittgenstein's theory of meaning, and the third part (Chapters V and VI) deals with the problems of negation and negative facts, and the theory of truth and falsehood (respectively). The general plan of the argument may be outlined chapter by chapter as follows.

Chapter I consists of a discussion of a few of the most funda-

[2] Perhaps I should add here that the bulk of this book was completed in the winter of 1964. Hence it does not take into account any material published since that time.

mental ideas of Wittgenstein's ontology. It approaches these ideas via the distinction between facts and objects by asking why Wittgenstein holds that the world consists of facts and not objects. This in turn leads to a preliminary discussion of their nature and relationship. It concludes with a few brief indications about the relationship between ontology and language, which leads into the discussion of meaning in Chapters II-IV.

Chapter II attempts to explain the function of objects (or substance) in Wittgenstein's theory of meaning, especially in terms of the notion of the sense (*Sinn*) of propositions and the nature of names and the role they play in language. In particular, I am concerned with demonstrating why objects and names are necessary conditions for the sense of propositions, and are hence presupposed by theory of meaning. The second part of this chapter consists of an interpretation of the nature of elementary propositions. Three questions will be raised: Are elementary propositions sense-data statements; Are sense-data objects; Are properties, concepts, or relations objects?[3] The discussion of the latter constitutes the beginning of the treatment of the picture theory of meaning.

Chapter III is concerned with the nature of the picture theory of meaning. The first part is a discussion of the notion of language as a picture, with emphasis on the concepts of logical form, structure, and pictorial form. Here the problem of the relationship between picture and fact is raised, concluding with detailed criticisms of some of the more important and influential views of the picture theory of meaning expressed by some of its critics.

Chapter IV deals with logical form, mysticism, and the distinction between saying (*sagen*) and showing (*zeigen*). It begins with a general discussion of the nature of logical and philosophical analysis. The main emphasis of this chapter falls on the problem

[3] One of my main reasons for treating these particular questions in detail was the tendency of philosophers to see the *Tractatus* as a representative of logical positivism. I believe this to be fundamentally misleading and to have resulted in the obscuring of some of the most typical and important of Wittgenstein's early philosophical views. Fortunately, there are signs that this tendency has substantially abated in recent years.

of the nature of logical form and its place in the picture theory of meaning. This gives rise to a discussion of the distinction between saying and showing and the mystical. The central problem in regard to the latter is seen to be the determination of the limits to what can be said both about the world and about language itself. Included are references to the position of Carnap, the "third Man" argument, self-reference, and the infinite regress.

Chapter V, which deals with the problems of negation and negative facts, is a preliminary to the discussion of the theory of truth in Chapter VI. It attempts to explain Wittgenstein's views on negative facts in terms of his doctrine that every elementary proposition has one and only one negation. My basic contention is that the former and the latter are basically two aspects of the *same* doctrine. In order to show this I have discussed the notions of logical space and place, together with a criticism of alternatives to Wittgenstein's position suggested by Demos and Russell.

Chapter VI deals with Wittgenstein's theory of truth and falsehood. This centers on the view that every significant elementary proposition can be either true or false. Thus, the relationship between sense and truth is brought out, followed by the relationship between falsehood and negative facts. The chapter concludes with an exposition of Wittgenstein's "correspondence" theory of truth, and of what such correspondence consists.

In the Conclusion I call attention to what I believe to be the most important results of my interpretation. I then discuss such general problems as Wittgenstein's conception of philosophy, his doctrine of solipsism, and his mysticsm. Finally, I offer a general criticism of the *Tractatus* as a whole. This critisism stems from the apparent self-refuting character of the work, and focuses upon Wittgenstein's seeming inability to justify the possibility of philosophical thought and expression.

Finally, I would like to add that at the time I decided to write this book I did so in the belief that it is one of the most significant philosophical works of our century, and that this significance had not been sufficiently understood and appreciated. I still believe this, though I no longer have the same sympathy with its content, aims and methods, partly for the reasons given in the Conclusion of this work.

I would like to express my gratitude to my friend and former teacher, Professor Henry W. Johnstone, Jr. Though I have always profited greatly from talking with him about philosophy, my debt is especially great in regard to the present work.

TABLE OF CONTENTS

Preface 9

I. Objects and Facts 17

II. Objects and Elementary Propositions 30

III. The Picture Theory of Meaning 44

IV. Meaning, Logical Form, and Mysticism 65

V. Negation and Negative Facts 89

Negation. 90

Negative Facts 102

VI. Truth and Falsehood 110

Conclusion. 128

Selected Bibliography 146

1

OBJECTS AND FACTS

The world is the totality of facts, not of things. (1.1)[1]

My main intentions in this chapter are threefold. First, I wish to draw attention to some of the more important characteristics of Wittgestein's ontology,[2] or his views on the nature of non-linguistic reality. This consists of a discussion of the *nature* of facts and objects, and their relationship to each other. I do not aim at completeness, since what is said here can only be fully understood in the light of Wittgenstein's philosophy of language. The latter, under the dual aspects of meaning and truth, constitutes the remainder of this book. Thus, what I have to say about facts and objects in this chapter is essentially introductory and provisional. Second, I will begin my discussion of Wittgenstein's theory of names. This will be done solely within the context of the theory of objects. In particular, I want to sketch the *relationship* between names and objects. The actual *function* of the name in theory of meaning will be taken up in Chapters II and III. Third, I wish to show in general terms the essential interdependency between philosophy of language and ontology in Wittgenstein's thought, and how the former determines the basic structure of the latter.

[1] This and all subsequent direct quotations from the text of the *Tractatus Logico-Philosophicus* will be taken from the Pears-McGuinness translation (London, Routledge & Kegan Paul, 1961). Each quotation will be followed by its corresponding section number in the text in parentheses.

[2] The use of the term "ontology" is not a completely happy one, but I retain it for want of a better word. The problem is that, strictly speaking, the theory of meaning of the *Tractatus* renders all "ontological statements" meaningless. Nevertheless, Wittgenstein does indeed have an "ontology". (See my concluding chapter). At this point, may it suffice to warn the reader that its meaning in the context of the *Tractatus* is very different from many of its more traditional associations.

The above three problems can be stated in the form of three questions. (1) What does it mean to say that the world consists of facts and not things (objects)? (2) What would it be *like* for the world to consist of things? (3) Assuming the possibility that the world consists of things could we *say* anything about such a world, i.e., describe it? I will begin by making a few general remarks on the overall structure and content of the *Tractatus*.

It is well-known that there are seven major statements or "propositions" in the *Tractatus* (designated in the text by the whole numbers 1-7). All other statements are intended to be subsidiary to these and to be explications and expansions of the thoughts expressed in them. The relative importance of each of the subsidiary statements or paragraphs is indicated by the decimal numbering device specially adopted by Wittgenstein for this purpose.[3] The fact that these seven major statements are distributed throughout the book makes it clear that the formal structure of the *Tractatus* is not modelled on that of a deductive system. That is, the opening statements are in no sense to be thought of as "axioms" or definitions from which the latter ones are deduced as "theorems". The opening pages in no way serve as "proofs" of what is said in the later ones. This rather obvious fact has one important consequence which may be overlooked, namely, that as far as the argument is concerned the *Tractatus* does not have to be *read* in the same order as it is *written*, i.e., from the beginning to the end. Rather, we may read it backwards, beginning with statement 7 and ending with statement 1. In fact, I think that ultimately it is indifferent where one begins to read the *Tractatus*, for one will always come back to the same "place".[4]

[3] Ludwig Wittgenstein, *Tractatus Logico-Philosophicus* (London, Routledge & Kegan Paul, 1961), p. 7 footnote. How seriously one is to take this convention is another matter. I myself doubt its reliability as a guide in *all* cases. The point I wish to make, however, is that this is the way Wittgenstein chose to express his thoughts, and that in studying him we should not disregard this, but rather try to see *why* he did so, and what its implications might be.

[4] Schopenhauer made an analogous claim for his own philosophy when he said that everything he had written was intended to be the explication of a *single* idea. Arthur Schopenhauer, *The World as Will and Representation* (Indian Hills, Colorado, Falcon's Wing Press, 1958), p. xx. Thus, where one

Keeping the above in mind let us look at the general structure of the *Tractatus* and see what this reveals about its *content*. The last statement of the book says:

What we cannot speak about we must consign to silence (7).

This expression is remarkably similar to what Wittgenstein says in the Preface about the ultimate "sense" (*Sinn*) of the *Tractatus*.

The whole sense of the book might be summed up in the following words: what can be said at all can be said clearly, and what we cannot talk about we must consign to silence.[5]

The *Tractatus* now begins to assume a kind of circular form . What is expressed as a conclusion is at the same time expressed as the intention of the work. This idea is a kind of "*leitmotiv*" which dominates the thought from beginning to end. We thus come back to where we started, although, as in Wagner's "Tristan und Isolde", the chord constituting the major *leitmotiv* (the "Tristan chord") is not "resolved" until the very end. Similarly, Wittgenstein's major thought (statement 7) is not *expressed* until the end, though it is constantly present, guiding and structuring the whole.

Looking at the *Tractatus*' content in more detail one sees that the first two major statements (1 and 2) are concerned with non-linguistic reality (ontology), and the last five with language. Assuming that it is possible to read the *Tractatus* both forwards and backwards we get an important clue to the relationship between language and reality in Wittgenstein's philosophy. That is, if it does not matter whether we begin with his views on facts and objects, or with those on language, it is clear that the two are essentially related and interdependent, the nature of the one determining that of the other. Let us see in more detail what this means by turning to the discussion of the first problem raised at the beginning of this chapter.

---

begins to read is indifferent, as long as one reads everything. In Wittgenstein there are seven "main ideas", although from one point of view these could be reduced to one, namely, statement 7. (Cite *Tractatus*, p. 3).

[5] Wittgenstein, *op. cit.*, p. 3.

The two major statements about non-linguistic reality are:

The world is all that is the case. (1)

What is the case — a fact [*Tatsache*] — is the existence of states of affairs [*Sachverhalten*]. (2)[6]

The first amplification of 1 is: "The world is the totality of facts, not of things" (1.1). The above dichotomy between facts (*Sachverhalte*) and things (*Dinge*, or *Gegenstände*)[7] lies at the heart of Wittgenstein's ontology. We must therefore return to the first question proposed in this chapter, What does it mean to say that the world consists of facts and not things? This idea is no doubt paradoxical to the common sense mind. The latter thinks of the world as a kind of empty "box" which is filled by all kinds of different "things", like tables, trees, clouds, can-openers, and even persons. Facts are somehow important and are often talked about, e.g., by detectives and businessmen, but it is odd to say the world "consists", is "made up" of them.

One of the first things we must realize in trying to understand Wittgenstein's "paradoxical" position is that he does not hold that the world consists of facts *because* they are simple and unanalyzable. The slightest acquaintance with the *Tractatus* shows us that the reverse is really the case — the world consists of facts because they are *complex*. The corollary to this is that objects cannot "make up" the world precisely because they are *simple*. With this we can understand Wittgenstein's rejection of reductive analysis and his break with what I choose to call the Hume-Russell tradition of philosophical analysis. Russell, for example, envisaged one of the essential tasks of metaphysics to be a "description" of the ultimate constituents of the world. The latter were arrived at by

[6] The implied difference between a *Tatsache* and a *Sachverhalt* seems to be that the latter is an *existent* fact (*Tatsache*). It is also logically unanalysable into other more elementary facts.

[7] It is interesting to note that "*Gegenstand*" is a compound of the two words "*gegen*" and "*standen*", which together literally mean "to stand against" or "to stand opposed to". Thus, when Wittgenstein says (Cf. 2.01) that a state of affairs (*Sachverhalt*) is a combination (*Verbindung*) of objects, this means literally that, in the state of affairs, the objects "stand opposed" to one another.

the method of reductive analysis, which roughly consisted of seeking what is simple (i.e., not susceptible to further logical analysis) by a process of logically separating out the elements composing the complex. When this "reduction" to the simple is accomplished the complex can be seen as a logical "construction" out of the simple. The assumption behind this whole attempt was that what is logically simple is identical with what is metaphysically or ontologically simple. In addition, logical and ontological simplicity, the basis of the *being* of the world, are the ultimate elements of our *knowledge* of the world. Wittgenstein, however, rejects this position by denying the identity between logical and ontological simplicity, and by grounding being in complexity. Knowledge (in the sense of *that which* is knowable) and being are both in the realm of the complex. Thus, the complex — the fact — is that which can exist in itself (has being) and that which can be known, or talked about. On the other hand, the simple — the object — can neither exist in itself nor be known. In order to get clearer on what this means let us return to the Hume-Russell tradition.

For (say) Hume the complex is a "construction" out of the logically and ontologically simple. This construction is essentially psychological and is termed custom or habit. What is "given" to the mind is the simple impression, which is known either through external sense-perception or by introspection (as in the case of feelings, or emotions). From these impressions the mind abstracts "ideas", which are "copies" of their respective original impressions.[8] By means of the psychological mechanism of habit both the external world, including material objects themselves and their relations (e.g., causality and contiguity), and the self or mind are constructed. A physical object, then, is a collection or "bundle" of impressions, the latter being its "parts". (A physical object is really a class of which the impressions are members.) The simple is thus a con-

[8] David Hume, *A Treatise on Human Nature*, Vol. I (New York, E. P. Dutton & Co. Inc., 1961), p. 11 *passim*. This also served as the basis of Hume's theory of meaning. Thus, for him theory of meaning, epistemology, and ontology all have the same common basis, namely, the "impression". For Wittgenstein, however, these three areas are radically divorced from one another.

stituent of the complex in the same sense as a part is a constituent of the whole.[9]

For Wittgenstein, however, the relationship between the simple and the complex — the object and the fact — is not thought of in terms of the part-whole distinction. Objects are not "parts" of facts, even though the latter are "combinations" (*Verbindungen*) of objects (2.01). What then, is the relationship between a fact and its constituent objects? To answer this question, I will turn to a discussion of the nature of objects.

Perhaps the most striking characteristic of the object is that it lacks all *material* properties. This is connected with the position that objects are identical with substance (*Substanz*), both in nature and function, as we see from the following.

> Objects make up the substance of the world. That is why they cannot be composite. (2.021)
>
> The substance of the world *can* only determine a form, and not any material properties. For it is only by means of propositions that material properties are represented — only by the configuration of objects that they are produced. (2.0231)

This introduction of the notion of substance in connection with objects is extremely significant. Often throughout the history of philosophy substance has been taken to be precisely that which constituted the formal properties of the world. From Aristotle to Hume it was the logical and metaphysical "ground" of the world's material properties, the "*substratum*" in which the latter were said to "inhere". When separated from its material properties by logical analysis it was purely formal or abstract. Being purely formal, substance was felt by many philosophers, in particular those in the empiricist tradition, to be a vague abstraction of the mind. But it was still believed by some to be both a necessity of

[9] I mean to imply by this that an impression is a "part" of a material object only in so far as it is considered philosophically as "constructed" out of impressions. Outside this context, for instance on the level of naive common sense, a "part" of a physical object, say a table, would be a leg, its top, or a drawer, etc.

thought and a necessity of being. Even this, however, was not given as a sufficient reason for maintaining that substance is "real" in the sense that it is that of which the world is *composed*. Hence, Aristotle gives another definition of substance, which he calls primary substance (*ousia*), as that which is said to be real in that it alone can exist independently as a self-contained entity. Primary substance is an individual, concrete existent, with characteristics which distinguish it from all other individuals. But substance, in thus becoming real, independent, and concrete lost its simplicity. It became a complex of two other elements, form and matter, each of which, though simple *in* themselves could not exist independently *by* themselves, but only in union with one another. Thus, Aristotle makes a clear distinction between that which can exist by itself as ontologically real and that which can exist only in thought, or that which can be separated in the mind and not in reality. The result is that what is simple in thought is not necessarily simple in reality, i.e., can exist independently *qua* simple. Primary substances are thus ontologically real but are not logically simple.

This denial of the thesis that the simple in thought is necessarily the simple in reality is, as we have seen, at the basis of Wittgenstein's doctrine that the world consists of facts, not things. Facts are logically complex, but they alone can be said to "make-up" the world, just as Aristotle's primary substance, though logically (and ontologically) complex, can alone be said to "make up" reality.[10]

So much (at least for the present) for the *nature* of objects and their relationship to facts. Let us now see what the ontological *function* of the object is.[11] Here again a parallel with Greek philosophy may prove illuminating. For Wittgenstein, the object is conceived as the "unalterable form" of the world.

[10] "The thing is not an existent out of which atomic facts could be constructed, it is an instrument of logical analysis and can be defined only as the possibility of a fact". G. D. O'Brien, "*Meaning and Fact: A Study in the Philosophy of Wittgenstein*", unpublished doctoral dissertation, University of Chicago, 1960.

[11] The function of objects in the theory of meaning will be taken up in Chapter II.

It is obvious that an imagined world, however different it may be from the real one, must have *something* — a form — in common with it. (2.022)

Objects are just what constitute this unalterable form (2.023). Thus, for Wittgenstein, objects or substance serves as the unchanging ground or basis amid constant change. Outside substance, i.e., in the realm of facts, all is "accident" (6.41). The objects are the "fixed form" of the world (2.026). This is analogous to the role substance played in Greek philosophy, where substance was the fixed form of the world in terms of which it was possible to explain change; in particular, how a thing could assume contrary properties, that is, *become* what it "is" not.

The identification of objects with substance and the insistence on an unchanging *form* amid the constant "flux" of facts also serves to emphasize the importance of *possibility* in Wittgenstein's thought. What is actual at any given time — the totality of existent states of affairs (*Sachverhalte*) — does not exhaust the realm facts (*Tatsachen*). As a corollary to this, *which* state of affairs exists is not determined (logically) by the nature of the world, and since these determine the nature of the world, by any other state of affairs (2.062).

The notion of possibility in regard to objects gives us a clue as to why they cannot determine the world. What the world *is* must be actual, but

It is essential to things that they should be possible constituents of states of affairs. (2.011)

The distinguishing characteristic of an object is that it *can* enter into a fact, that is, that it intrinsically possesses the possibility of constituting an actual existent, a fact. The fact is the expression of the material properties of the world, and it is through their union in a fact that objects are able to constitute a world (2.0231). The term "object" does not stand for any actual and existent thing or class of things in the world. (To paraphrase Wittgenstein, if we went around in the world looking for an object we would not find one.) In other words, "object" is a pseudo-concept. It is not a *name*, and thus cannot be substituted for the variable in a propositional function. Rather, it is simply the blank *space* normally filled by a variable, i.e., the (#) in the expression Ø(x). The name of an *existent* entity would fill the space (or replace the variable), and since the concept of object is really nothing but the space *itself, it* cannot be such a substitution instance.

We are now in a position to answer the second question raised in this chapter, namely, "What would it be *like* for the world to consist of things (objects)?" But in order to do so it is necessary to make a few preliminary remarks on Wittgenstein's theory of names. These remarks will be developed in much greater detail in the following chapters on meaning, but a rough beginning is indispensable at this point.

A basic principle of Wittgenstein's doctrine of language is that names, being the simple elements of sentences, are the linguistic correlatives of objects (propositions being the linguistic correlative of facts). When we "speak" of objects, therefore, we *name* them. We cannot, for instance, describe or assert an object; strictly speaking, we cannot talk *about* objects at all, for to name a thing is not to "talk about" it — in the sense of describing it — but merely linguistically to "point it out", or designate it (3.221). What we describe, assert, and talk about are facts. Thus, assuming that the world consists of objects and not facts we would have to conclude, on the basis of the above remarks on names, that such a world would not be *like* anything at all, for it would have no qualities. Here I mean material qualities (/) as opposed to purely formal ones (/), for example, color (Cf. 2.0231, 2.0232). But the former are what constitute a *world,* i.e., the realm of the actual, concrete, and existent. A "world" of purely formal properties, that is, of objects alone, would be a mere "realm of possibility". As a realm of possibility it could not constitute a world, but would be merely a necessary *condition* for one — a "place" in a logical sense. A "world" of objects is therefore ultimately self-contradictory, for the concept of a world presupposes the existence of material properties, the latter being what the object *apart* from the fact cannot provide.

Material properties of the world are "produced" (*gebildet*) by the configuration (*Konfiguration*) of objects *within* the fact, not from objects considered by themselves (Cf. 2.0231).

We are now in a position to answer our third question, Could we *say* anything about a "world" of objects alone? It is obvious from what has been said so far that the answer is decidedly negative. Wittgenstein's doctrine of names asserts that the object can only be named, and that to name an object is not to *say* anything *about* it. If, *per impossible*, we could say anything about an object what we would be talking about would be no longer an object but a fact, and our "talking about" would be no longer naming but describing or asserting by means of propositions. A world which consisted solely of objects could only be named, and this would not constitute significant discourse, just as a world of objects does not constitute a genuine world. Our process of naming would tell us neither *how* the world is nor *what* it is.[12] The ultimate unit of significant discourse, then, is the proposition. It is *only* by means of propositions that we can say anything about the world.

The ontological corollary of this is that the world consists of facts because only facts can be the subject-matter of significant discourse. We assert facts, or more specifically, the existence and non-existence of *Sachverhalte* (2), by means of propositions, and in doing so we say "what is the case", or "how the world is". We cannot say anything significant about *how* the world is by naming objects. The name tells us only *that* the world is, for the existence of a name presupposes the existence of its bearer, the object, which is its meaning (*Bedeutung*) (3.203). But *that* the world is is the mystical (6.522). The sentence, "A exists" (where "A" is a logically proper name) *says* nothing about the world. It is nonsensical (*unsinnig*) because the name "A" itself presupposes the existence of its bearer, and hence it is grammatically incorrect and redundant to predicate existence of it. We could tell by merely

[12] Strictly speaking, for Wittgenstein such a process of naming is impossible, for a name can only function as a *name* in the context of a proposition, and not by itself. In addition, it will be remembered that for Aristotle the answer to the question, "What is it?" is "Substance", i.e., primary substance. Thus, he too recognized *complexity* as a necessary condition for significant discourse.

looking at the sentence that it is "true", i.e., designates its object. But for Wittgenstein the truth of a significant proposition (one with *Sinn*) can never be determined from the proposition itself, but only by reference to the reality which it pictures and which lies outside it.[13]

Since we cannot significantly predicate existence of a name, and names are the designators of objects, we cannot *say* of an object that it exists, or indeed describe it in any way.[14] Logical simplicity, though a *condition* for significant discourse, cannot by itself *constitute* it. Significant discourse begins at the level of complexity, that is, with the proposition. Moreover, the existence of *one* fact can neither be a world nor the subject of significant discourse, for the world is what we speak about, and speaking about presupposes at least *two* facts, one of which can serve as the picture of the other (2.1, 2.141). Thus, we see that linguistic and ontological complexity go hand-in-hand with pluralism.

The world is all that is the case. (1)
What is the case — a fact — is the existence of states of affairs. (2)

In the *Notebooks* Wittgenstein asks the following rhetorical question:

Suppose there is something outside the *facts!* Which our propositions are impotent to express? But here we do have, e.g., *things* [*Dinge*] *and we feel no demand at all* to express them in propositions.[15]

Here, I think, we can get a glimpse of at least the *spirit* behind Wittgenstein's assertion that the world consists of facts. In effect he is saying that even *if* there were entities of some kind which

[13] F. P. Ramsey, *The Foundations of Mathematics* (Paterson, New Jersey, Littlefield, Adams & Co., 1960), p. 281.
[14] It is obvious that in science one often asserts or denies existence, but, strictly speaking, this can only be done in the case of *descriptions*, and not logically proper names. This is largely a technical result of Russell's analysis of descriptions, which, of course, Wittgenstein at this time accepted, at least in broad outline.
[15] Ludwig Wittgenstein, *Notebooks 1914-1916*, ed. G. E. M. Anscombe and G. H. von Wright (Oxford, Basil Blackwell, 1961), p. 51e.

were not facts these would be of no "interest" to us. We must remember that Wittgenstein's concern in the *Tractatus* is with the necessary conditions for the meaningfulness of cognitive or scientific discourse (analogous to Kant's interest in the *Critique* with the necessary conditions for the possibility of *knowledge*).

Therefore, he is concerned with the nature of the proposition, the basic unit of such discourse, and this in turn focuses his attention on the nature of the fact. The *Tractatus* is concerned with what can be significantly said, i.e., what can be true or false, what can tell us something about the world. And since propositions tell us how the world is, what is of importance about the world is just that it can be seen to consist of facts. Outside the facts nothing can be said and hence nothing can be known. *The world consists of facts because this is all that can be said about it.* In the discussion of objects and naming we have seen that any attempt to go beyond propositions and facts results in neither a significant language nor a world.

It is now possible to summarize the major conclusions reached in this chapter. The assertion that the world consists of facts and not things is seen to be justified on two grounds. First, things (objects) lack all material properties and hence cannot constitute a world, the latter being necessarily concrete and existent. The object has only formal properties, and has reference to the realm of possibility rather than actuality. Second, even the *assumption* of the possibility of a world of objects proves futile, because nothing can be *said* about it. This follows mainly from Wittgenstein's doctrine of names. Also, we have seen that the relation of objects to facts is not that of part to whole. Wittgenstein's break with the Hume-Russell tradition of reductive analysis is made possible by radically distinguishing between logical and ontological simplicity, such that the logically simple is not *identical* with the ontologically simple, the latter being that out of which the world is composed and that which can exist by itself. Thus, the object is a necessary *condition* for the possibility of the world but cannot be said to *constitute* it.

Finally, we saw the interdependence of language and reality, the former determining the nature of the latter in and through the delimitation of its own nature and function. Reality is what we can *say* it is, the nature of this saying being a function of the nature of language itself. We are thus led to the problem of meaning, which is the subject of the next chapter.

II

OBJECTS AND ELEMENTARY PROPOSITIONS

> If the world had no substance, then whether a proposition had sense would depend on whether another proposition was true. (2.0211)

I have two main purposes in this chapter. First, I wish to continue my exposition of Wittgenstein's theory of objects by showing their function in theory of meaning. That is, in this chapter I want to show how objects function as the ultimate determinates of sense (*Sinn*) in *language*. This will serve to amplify and complete my exposition of the doctrine of objects begun in Chapter I, where I was concerned with objects from an *ontological* point of view, both in regard to their own nature and their relationship to facts (*Sachverhalte*). In particular, the present discussion will attempt to uncover the relationship between meaning (*Sinn*) and truth by showing why Wittgenstein believes that objects are necessary *if* we are to understand the sense of propositions without knowing whether they are actually true. This will be illustrated first from a *negative* point of view by the theory of descriptions, as formulated by Russell. I hope to show that the possibility of radical falsehood in the case of description-sentences proves that there must be at least *some* propositions for which such falsehood is *not* possible, i.e., there must be propositions consisting solely of logically proper names and not descriptions. By this route, objects are seen to be necessary presuppositions of theory of meaning, since only objects can be the references (*Bedeutungen*) of logical names.

Once the necessity of objects and names is proven I will be able to undertake my second major purpose in this chapter, namely, the beginning of my exposition of the doctrine of elementary propositions (*Elementarsätze*). In particular, I wish to show *why* the latter (like objects and names) are necessary presuppositions in

Wittgenstein's theory of meaning. This will develop out of the previous analysis of descriptions, names, and objects. I will begin my treatment of the *nature* of elementary propositions by asking three questions: Are Wittgenstein's elementary propositions sense-data statements; Are sense-data objects; Are properties, concepts or relations objects? The discussion of elementary propositions begun in this chapter furnishes the beginning of my exposition of elementary propositions. It will be completed in Chapter III where I deal with the picture theory of meaning proper.

In the previous chapter I discussed what I felt to be the basic characteristics of Wittgenstein's ontology and tried to indicate some of the reasons why he holds the views he does. In particular, I was concerned with why Wittgenstein asserts that the world consists of facts and not things. I said that although things are not the "ultimate constituents" of the world they are nonetheless necessary conditions for the possibility of such constituents.

> Each thing is, as it were, in a space of possible states of affairs [*Sachverhalte*]. This space I can imagine empty, but I cannot imagine the thing [*Ding*] without the space. (2.013)
>
> A spatial object must be situated in infinite space. (A spatial point is an argument-place). (2.0131)

This passage, which is reminiscent of Kant's argument for the ideality and transcendental character of space and time in the Transcendental Aesthetic of the *Critique of Pure Reason*,[1] draws an analogy between physical space and spatial objects and states of affairs and objects. Just as, for Kant, space is a necessary condition for the possibility of the existence of spatial objects (the latter being inconceivable without the former), so for Wittgenstein the fact (*Sachverhalt*) is a necessary condition for the possibility of the object (*Gegenstand*). The *Sachverhalt* is the "logical space"[2] into

[1] Immanuel Kant, *Critique of Pure Reason*, 2nd ed., trans. by N. K. Smith (London, MacMillan & Co. Ltd., 1961), p. 68 ff.

[2] It will be remembered (Cite Introduction) that a *Tatsache* is a *possible Sachverhalt*. The former is a possible fact whereas the latter is always actual. This is analogous to the distinction between *sensibilia* and sense-data.

which an object may enter, and in doing so it becomes a constituent of that *Sachverhalt*, just as the spatial object becomes a constituent of physical space by occupying a point (or "place") in it.

The argument for the ontological reality of objects is thus *a priori*; objects are not "given" in experience. If they were they would not be objects but facts. In short, objects are an *a priori* necessity in ontology for the possibility of *facts*; similarly, in theory of meaning they are an *a priori* necessity for the possibility of *sense*.

If the world had no substance, then whether a proposition had sense would depend on whether another proposition was true. (2.0211)

In that case we could not sketch out any picture of the world, true or false. (2.0212)

Why does Wittgenstein assert in 2.0211 that objects are necessary conditions for the possibility of a proposition's having sense? Wittgenstein says that the question of the possibility of a proposition's having sense is intimately connected with the problem of showing how a proposition can have meaning *independently* of a prior determination of that or any other proposition's truth-value.

This connection can be well illustrated, I think, albeit in a negative fashion, by a consideration of Russell's theory of descriptions[3] which, of course, had a great influence on Wittgenstein. The main purpose of Russell's theory was to show how a sentence containing a description (i.e., a phrase of the form: the so-and-so) could be both meaningful and false even though the object denoted by the description-phrase might not exist. The solution was found in showing that the description is not the real (i.e., logical) subject of the sentence, and that when the sentence is fully analyzed this phrase does not appear in it. Rather, it is replaced by variables. The result of the analysis is that the ostensible subject (the description-phrase) of the sentence drops out and the sentence becomes a quantified conjunction containing only variables. (The variable may then be replaced by a logically proper name *if* the sentence is found to be true.) In this way, Russell showed how a proposition

[3] Bertrand Russell, "On Denoting", in *Logic and Knowledge* (London, George Allen & Unwin Ltd., 1956), pp. 34-56.

whose subject does not designate an actual existent entity could be false and not simply meaningless. There was no longer any necessity for posting the existence (or "subsistence") of "metaphysical entities" in order to account for the meaningfulness of such propositions. This was believed to be a great step forward for both logic, and, in the theory's later application to reductive analysis, for epistemology and metaphysics.

One of the most important results of this analysis of descriptions is that a sentence containing a description-phrase can be false in either of *three* ways. Let us take as an example the sentence, "The present king of France is bald." (Here, of course, the phrase "the present King of France" is the description.) Russell's analysis makes the sentence read: (Ex) [x is a present king of France & (y) (y is a present king of France $\supset$ y = x) & x is bald]. The three possible ways this sentence may be false are the following. (1) There exists no object answering the description; (2) there exists more than one object answering the description; (3) the predicate ascribed to the object does not hold of it. Now, by grouping (1) and (2) together there result *two* basically distinct ways a description-sentence can be false, one having to do with the *existence* of the object and the other with its *properties*. The first way, which Anscombe[4] calls "radical falsehood", is when either condition (1) or condition (2) is not fulfilled. That is, when it is not the case that one and only one object answering to the description exists. The second way, which Anscombe calls "ordinary falsehood", is when, although both conditions (1) and (2) are fulfilled (i.e., there exists one and only one object), the predicate ascribed to the object does not hold. (Thus, although there may be one and only one x who is the present king of France this x may not be bald.) Having reduced the possible ways a description-sentence may be false to two by means of the distinction between radical and ordinary falsehood we see that it is the essence of such sentences that they can be false in one or both of these ways. Conversely, for them to be *true* both kinds of falsehood must be *lacking*. That

[4] G. E. M. Anscombe, *An Introduction to Wittgenstein's Tractatus* (London, Hutchinson University Library, 1959), p. 49 ff.

is, one and only one object must exist and it must possess the properties ascribed to it by the predicate.

The distinction between radical and ordinary falsehood parallels another distinction made by Anscombe between internal and external negation.[5] These are the two ways a non-elementary proposition can be *negated.* For example, the sentence, "The present king of France is bald" can be negated *externally* by denying it as a whole, i.e., by writing "Not: The present king of France is bald." This locution, in Anscombe's usage, claims that the sentence is *radically* false in that it denies that there exists one and only one entity denoted by the phrase, "the present king of France". On the other hand, it can be negated *internally* by writing "The present king of France is not bald." Here one is denying the ascription of the property baldness, rather than denying the existence of the present king of France. Thus, the sentence which is internally denied has *ordinary* falsehood. Therefore, there is always an ambiguity in the falsehood of sentences containing descriptions, and this ambiguity is an essential characteristic of such sentences. The logical structure of the sentence itself does not (and cannot) tell us *which* of the ways the sentence is false (if in fact it is false).

Now, the ambiguity of falsehood in the case of descriptions has serious consequences for the theory of meaning. The possibility of *radical* falsehood, which is always present, implies that we can never determine whether a given description-sentence is *true* unless we know that another sentence is true. For instance, take the sentence, "The candidate who gets the most votes will be elected." We can know that this sentence is true although we do not know *which* of the candidates will actually win the election; we know *that* one of the candidates will be elected although we cannot at present designate who it will be. But the possibility of knowing that this sentence is true is in turn dependent on knowing that there do in fact exist certain specifiable individuals who are the candidates. Thus, its truth depends on the actuality of the truth of some other sentence or sentences which make this designation, i.e., which explicitly assert *that* such individuals exist. In other

[5] *Ibid.*, p. 34.

words, in the case of a true description we know that there is *an* x satisfying the function although we do not know which, i.e., a, or b, or c, etc. But *one* of these must exist, and hence there must be *another* true sentence which asserts this. We are here in danger of a regress, perhaps an infinite one, for we are unable to determine the truth of a given statement without determining that of another. This, then, is the problem Wittgenstein's theory of objects is designed to solve.

For Wittgenstein, *if* a proposition is capable of radical falsehood it has no definite *sense*, since the sense of a proposition presupposes the possibility of determining its truth, i.e., of stating its truth-grounds.

> ... In order to say, '"*p*" is true (or false),' I must have determined in what circumstances I call '*p*' true, and in so doing I determine the sense of the proposition. (4.063)

The possibility of the definite sense (*Sinn*) of a proposition depends on the *im*possibility that at least *some* propositions are capable of radical falsehood, and this impossibility in turn depends on the existence of simple objects that can only be named.

> The requirement that simple signs be possible is the requirement that sense be determinate. (3.23)

A simple sign is by definition the name of a simple object (*Gegenstand*).

> Objects can only be *named.* Signs are their representatives. I can only speak *about* them: I cannot *put them into words.* (3.221)

Further, names lack sense (*Sinn*); they have only a reference (*Bedeutung*).

> A name means [*bedeutet*] an object. The object [*Gegenstand*] is its meaning [*Bedeutung*]. (3.203)[6]

[6] This doctrine marks one of Wittgenstein's most radical breaks with Frege. For Frege, a name has both *Sinn* and *Bedeutung*, just as a proposition has both *Sinn* and *Bedeutung*. For Wittgenstein, however, names have only *Bedeutung*, and propositions have only *Sinn*. Thus, he broke down Frege's parallel between propositions and names. (See Gottlob Frege, *Translations from the Philosophical Writings of Gottlob Frege*, ed. by P. Geach and M. Black (Oxford, Basil Blackwell, 1960), esp. "On Sense and Reference".

And finally, and this is crucial, the mere *existence* of a logically proper name presupposes the actual existence of its object or bearer. If an object has a name, *a fortiori*, the object exists. To use a name in a proposition presupposes that the object the name designates exists; or again, the use of a name in a proposition presupposes that the name has a *Bedeutung*, for a (logically proper) name without a *Bedeutung* is self-contradictory. (The reader must remember that a name-sign functions as a name only in the context of a proposition (3.3); it is meaningless to talk of a "name" by itself outside this context.)

Now we can see an alternative to the dilemma posed by radical falsehood in the case of descriptions. This alternative lies in the ontological presupposition of simple objects, and the existence of simple signs or names for these objects. A sentence containing such names will be incapable of radical falsehood because the very presence of the name logically entails the existence of its bearer. We thus do not need another true statement asserting the existence of this bearer, for the sentence itself "shows" (*zeigt*) this (Cf. 4.126).

The discussion of the theory of descriptions has served a twofold purpose. First, it illustrated the situation in which a proposition can be radically false. This illustration then led us to see that in the case of such sentences we must presuppose the existence of other statements which are *not* capable of radical falsehood, for it was the latter which determine the possibility of the former having a determinate sense. This does not mean, however, that Wittgenstein wished to dispense with descriptions altogether. It just means that descriptions cannot fulfill the function of naming that is demanded *if* propositions are to have sense independent of the truth-value of some other proposition (or propositions). And *this* in turn is necessary in order to avoid the possibility of an infinite regress, and because to know the sense of a proposition is simply to know what would be the case *if* it were true (4.024). Thus, we must presuppose names and objects in addition to descriptions. And finally, we saw that *only* sentences containing logically proper names could fulfill this function, and that such names designate simple objects. Objects are thus necessary presuppositions in

Wittgenstein's theory of meaning, for otherwise sentences would be capable of radical falsehood, and this in turn would imply that they would lack a determinate sense.

Having demonstrated the necessity of objects and names we have also shown the necessity for elementary propositions (*Elementarsätze*), since the latter are defined as mere "concatenations" of names.

An elementary proposition consists of names. It is a nexus, a concatenation, of names. (4.22)

It is only in the nexus of an elementary proposition that a name occurs in a proposition. (4.23)

Because names are necessary conditions for the possibility of the determinate sense of propositions, and elementary propositions are "concatenations" of names, the latter are also necessary presuppositions for determinate sense. Thus, we can understand the *sense* of an elementary proposition without knowing whether it is *actually* true.

To understand a proposition means to know what is the case if it is true.
(One can understand it, therefore, without knowing whether it is true).
It is understood by anyone who understands its constituents. (4.024)

In short, without elementary propositions it would be impossible both to understand the meaning of a given proposition and to determine its truth-value (just as was the case with names and objects). Thus, Wittgenstein's argument for elementary propositions is also *a priori* and purely logical — they are necessary conditions for the possibility of significant discourse, i.e., for talking about and asserting the existence of facts. This can be readily seen by observing that

... We can draw conclusions from a false proposition. This is the same fact as that we can invent or devise a proposition and know what it means, without first discovering the facts which hold in regard to its subject matter.[7]

That is, we can derive a valid conclusion whether the premisses are true *or* false, and without actually knowing which. All that is

[7] Anscombe, *op. cit.*, p. 31.

necessary is that we *assume* that the premisses are true, for in a valid argument we assert no more than that *if* the premisses are true the conclusion *must* be true. This is a familiar procedure, and would not be possible if we had to ascertain the actual truth of the premisses *before* making the deductions.[8] Indeed, this is roughly what a scientist does when considering an hypothesis. If it were not possible to draw conclusions from premisses without knowing that they are actually true the scientist would have to know that his hypothesis is true before he began investigating whether it was true or not, which of course would be absurd and vitiate the whole scientific enterprise. Having thus seen *why* Wittgenstein holds that elementary propositions are necessary we must go on to investigate the *nature* of such propositions. This in turn will enable us to examine in detail (in Chapter III) the picture theory of meaning itself.

I will begin my exposition by raising three questions. First, Are Wittgenstein's ultimate simples, the *Gegenstände*, sense-data, or conversely, are sense-data instances of *Gegenstände*; second, Is a statement of the form "This is red" or "This-red-here-now", which describes or reports a sense-datum (or sense-data), an instance of an *Elementarsatz*; and third, Are objects properties, concepts, or relations? Let me attempt to answer the first question by asking if a sense-datum is simple or unanalyzable, i.e., is it an object in Wittgenstein's sense? I think that the answer to this must be negative for the following reasons. For any given sense-datum, e.g., a red patch, we can always say without self-contradiction that it could have been blue, or green, etc. That is, *that* this-sense-datum-here-now is red is a contingent fact, one which could quite well have been otherwise. (By calling something "contingent" I mean simply that it can be denied without self-contradiction.) Though a visual sense-datum must have some color what color it in fact has (or is) is contingent. The occurrence of (say) a red sense-datum is, then,

[8] Of course, one can always demand that the premisses' truth be actually determined (either logically or empirically) in order to escape a supposed infinite regress. Also, the inference would not be a "proof" unless this condition were met. But these problems are not to the point here.

a *fact*.[9] As such, it cannot be an object in Wittgenstein's sense, and thus is complex and not simple. And sense-data, being complex and hence facts, cannot have names, and the statement "This is red" describes a red sense-datum, but does not *name* it. And conversely, since the sense-datum is not named, it is not an object, since objects and only objects are named. Finally, it will be remembered that for Wittgenstein "objects are colourless" (2.0232). This in itself is sufficient to prove that objects cannot be sense-data, for the latter, if they are visual ones, already have (or are) a given color.

An object is a *constituent* of a fact. It is not itself a fact, but rather is something which can occur in a specific *class* of facts. Further, what is essential to the object is that it be a *possible* constituent of a fact, not an actual constituent of an existing fact. In other words, since objects determine a range of possible facts by being intrinsically capable of entering into them as constituents they do not and cannot determine what *is* the case. At most they are necessary conditions for what is the case. But if objects were sense-data they themselves would *be* what is the case. For Wittgenstein, what is the case is always a fact and never an object.[10] In short, Wittgenstein believes that, in calling a sense-datum a simple, the analysis has not been carried far enough, for a sense-datum, *qua* sense-datum, is already a fact. It is a fact which can be further analyzed into its constituents, and it is only these latter that we can properly call simple objects.

It is essential to things [*dem Dinge*] that they should be possible constituents of states of affairs. (2.011)[11]

Second, Is a statement of the form "This is red", where "this" and "red" denote a sense-datum, an instance of an elementary proposition (*Elementarsatz*)? From the above argument against the identification of objects and sense-data we can see that, since

[9] Cf. J. O. Urmson, *Philosophical Analysis* (Oxford, Clarendon Press, 1956), p. 57.

[10] *Ibid*., p. 59.

[11] Wittgenstein implies in 2.01 that the three terms for object, "*Ding*", "*Gegenstand*", and "*Sache*" are synonomous.

a sense-datum is not an object, *ex hypothesi,* a statement describing or donoting a sense-datum cannot be an elementary proposition. Thus, the arguments of the first and second questions are correlative and support one another.

We now come to the third question. Since the sentence "This is red" contains a subject and a one-place predicate we may ask if predicates and or relations (two-place or more predicates) can properly be called names, and, correspondingly, whether properties and or relations can properly be called objects.[12] First, can properties be objects? The most obvious objection to this suggestion comes from 6.3751 where Wittgenstein says:

It is clear that the logical product of two elementary propositions can neither be a tautology nor a contradiction. The statement that a point in the visual field has two different colours at the same time is a contradiction. (6.3751)

If "This is red" is an elementary proposition then it cannot be contradicted by another elementary proposition. But it is clear from 6.3751 that to say "This is red" and "This is brown" — two distinct elementary propositions — where "this" refers to the *same* points in space and time, is a logical contradiction. "This is red", or any color-statement of the same form, therefore cannot be an instance of an elementary proposition. Again, one of the basic reasons why sense-data statements were taken as elementary and unanalyzable was that they supposedly denoted one and only one object. But this in itself shows that such statements cannot be instances of Wittgenstein's *Elementarsatz,* for the latter always represents a *configuration* of objects (3.21), which is the *Sachverhalt.*[13]

[12] Stenius explicitly states that properties and relations are objects. Erik Stenius, *Wittgenstein's Tractatus: A Critical Exposition of its Main Lines of Thought* (Oxford, Basil Blackwell, 1960), p. 70. Urmson implies that properties are objects, since he calls "This is red" an elementary proposition and the latter "observation" statements. Urmson, *op. cit.*, pp. 58, 60. Obviously, I disagree with both these views.

[13] Richard Bernstein, "Wittgenstein's Three Languages", *Review of Metaphysics*, XV, No. 2 (December 1961), p. 291 footnote.

Objects are without material or empirical properties ("objects are colourless" (2.0232)). *That* an object has, e.g., a color, is a *fact*. What is essential to the object is only that it *can* enter into a fact of a certain type. Now, it is obvious that the property red already has a material property, i.e., its redness, and that this fact can be *described*. Objects, on the other hand, can only be *named* (3.221). The doctrine that objects, and only objects, can be named leads to a further consequence which is fatal to the view that properties can be objects. It will be remembered that for Frege a concept (*Begriff*) was the reference (*Bedeutung*) of a predicate. Wittgenstein, however, denies this, asserting that there are no names of concepts, only of simples, and that therefore in a completely analyzed proposition there would be no signs for concepts.[14] Sentences of the form Ø(x) are *not* elementary propositions, and since "This is red" is a sentence of this form it cannot be an instance of such propositions. As to the question whether relations (as opposed to properties) can be objects I think we may also answer in the negative, since the above criticisms of properties as objects would also apply to relations of two or more places.[15]

> In Wittgenstein's fully analyzed proposition, we have nothing but a set of argument-places filled with names of objects; there seems to be no kind of expression that could be regarded as standing for a concept.[16]

Although propositions of the form Ø(x) cannot be elementary there is still the possibility that ones of the form Ø(x, y) could be, *if* (and only if) "Ø" is *not* a logically proper name and could therefore be eliminated in an *ideal* notation. And it seems impossible that the expression "Ø" in "Ø(x)" could be eliminated. And whether such signs *are* names is precisely the problem. I do not believe they are, partly for some of the reasons urged above against the view that predicates are names, and for other reasons

[14] Anscombe, *op. cit.*, pp. 99, 109.

[15] For additional arguments against the identification of objects and relations see Chapter III where I criticize Daitz, Evans, and Stenius on precisely this point.

[16] Anscombe, *op. cit.*, p. 110.

advanced below in Chapter III. Copi, however, while agreeing that propositions of the form Ø(x) are *not* elementary thinks that elementary propositions are *relational* and only relational, i.e., have *two* or more argument-places.[17] This, I think, is an important suggestion, and indeed *may* be true, if relation-signs are not names and thus could be eliminated in an ideal notation. Be this as it may, the essential point to realize is that for Wittgenstein there *must* be elementary propositions, of whatever form, and the question of *which* form these propositions have, albeit important, is secondary to this. But this much, at least, may be concluded at this point: objects are *not* sense-data, nor are they properties, concepts or relations.

It will be remembered that the two main problems raised in this chapter were (1) the function of objects in theory of meaning, and (2) the nature of elementary propositions. I believe that the following conclusions may now be drawn concerning their solution. First, objects are a necessary presupposition for theory of meaning because only by means of them is it possible for us to understand the sense (*Sinn*) of a proposition without knowing beforehand if it is true. Due to the possibility of radical falsehood, which is intrinsic to sentences containing descriptions, we can see that the latter, if they are true, always presuppose *another* (true) statement asserting that the entity satisfying the description exists. This points to the danger of a semantical regress unless there are *some* propositions which, by their very nature, cannot be radically false. This latter condition can only be met by a proposition consisting solely of logically proper names which necessarily have a reference (*Bedeutung*). In the case of such propositions then, we do not need to know another true statement asserting that there *is* an entity answering to the "name" or description. For Wittgenstein, this condition is crucial, for it must be possible to know the meaning (*Sinn*) of a proposition without referring to the truth of another proposition, or indeed, to any other proposition whatsoever. All

[17] I. M. Copi, "Objects, Properties and Relations in the *Tractatus*", *Mind*, LXVII, No. 266 (April 1958), p. 164.

we need to know is that the names have a reference, and this is satisfied by the theory of names and objects.

Having thus established the semantical function of objects, and shown that there are logical names, it was then possible to see that elementary *propositions* are also necessary presuppositions of theory of meaning, since elementary propositions are defined as consisting solely of names. This constituted the first step toward an exposition of the *nature* of elementary propositions, which was the second main problem of this chapter. I began this part of my discussion by raising the following three questions: (1) Are elementary propositions sense-data statements; (2) Are sense-data instances of objects; and (3) Are objects properties, concepts, or relations? Having found the answers to these each of these questions negative I conclude this part of my exposition of Wittgenstein's theory of elementary propositions. I will now continue by turning to the picture theory of meaning itself.

III

THE PICTURE THEORY OF MEANING

> There must be something identical in a picture and what it depicts, to enable the one to be a picture of the other at all. (2.161)

In Chapter II I raised the question of the nature of elementary propositions but tended to treat them from a rather negative point of view. Thus, for example, we saw that elementary propositions are not equivalent with sense-data statements, that their constituent elements (the names) do not designate sense-data, that objects are not sense-data, and also properties and relations are not objects. In this chapter I will continue my discussion of elementary propositions, but in more positive terms, and wholly within the context of the picture theory of meaning. In addition to my exposition of the picture theory of meaning I will enter into a critique of some of the commonest and most crucial misinterpretations of it. This criticism is undertaken, not for its own sake, but primarily in the hope that it will lead to a clearer understanding of the real nature of Wittgenstein's picture theory.

Thus, this chapter will revolve around one central idea, namely, the conception of elementary propositions as *pictures.* The point of departure will be the question: What are the essential characteristics of a picture, or What is it that makes an elementary proposition a picture? In the course of my discussion of this question the following points will be dealt with. (1) The fact that the picture (like the elementary proposition) consists of names. (2) The nature of the structure, pictorial form, and logical form of proposition-pictures. (3) The distinction between sign and symbol as applied to propositions. Second, I will attempt to elucidate what Wittgenstein means when he says that pictorial form constitutes the *possibility* of the picturing relation between picture and fact. This will lead to the problem of the isomorphism of picture and fact and the ideas of order and multiplicity. At this point I will begin my criticism. I will deal first with Daitz, Evans, and Stenius' attack on the "isomorphism" of pictures and facts. This will lead to a discussion of the nature of relations in the picture theory, and the traditional infinite regress argument against the reality of relations. Finally, I will conclude with a rather detailed critique of Daitz's general criticism of the picture theory of meaning. This critique is primarily aimed at exposing common misunderstandings of the latter, especially as it is found in the *Tractatus*. In this section three main problems will be raised: (1) Whether or not the picture theory is primarily applicable to words (and not sentences); (2) The relation of ordinary language to pictures; and (3) The place of *complex* propositions in the picture theory of meaning.

As I stated at the beginning of this chapter I plan to deal with the problem of the nature of elementary propositions by treating them in the context of the picture theory of meaning,[1] that is, as pictures of the world. This is justifiable, I think, because the elementary proposition (as opposed to complex propositions) is the basic unit of meaning (*Sinn*) in the *Tractatus*. Meaning is possible *because* the elementary proposition is a picture (*Bild*). However, it must be pointed out that Wittgenstein never *explicitly* identifies pictures with elementary propositions. When talking about propositions as pictures he uses the term "*Satz*" instead of "*Elementarsatz*". The former, having a wider meaning than "proposition" in its strictly logical sense, can also mean "sentence" or "statement". Nevertheless, on the basis of the general doctrines of the *Tractatus* I think it is obvious that *only* elementary propositions are pictures. (This will become clearer in the dis-

[1] Strictly speaking, Wittgenstein does not have a "theory" of meaning. This is one of the basic contentions of this book. I merely wish to assert it now in order to warn the reader and avoid possible misunderstanding. The reasons why this interpretation is correct, and what its significance is, can only be brought out later, primarily in Chapter IV.

cussion of complex propositions and the truth-functional nature of language in Chapter VI.) Having asserted that only elementary propositions are pictures let us turn to the place in the *Tractatus* where the picture theory first appears.

After asserting in 2 that "What is the case — a fact — is the existence of states of affairs" Wittgenstein at 2.1 turns from a consideration of the nature of the world to the realm of language, by saying:

We picture facts to ourselves. (2.1)[2]

What, then, are the distinguishing characteristics of a picture; what makes a picture a picture? First, a picture consists of names.

In a picture objects [*Gegenstande*] have the elements of the picture corresponding to them. (2.13)

In a picture the elements of the picture are the representatives of [*vertreten*] objects. (2.131)[3]

We see that (1) a picture consists of elements, and (2) that these elements "represent" (are "proxies" for) objects. Further,

The simple signs employed in propositions are called names. (3.202)[4]

But a proposition is not a mere *collection* of names, for names by themselves cannot express a sense, whereas the proposition can. "A proposition is articulated", i.e., the elements of the picture must be related in a certain *way* (3.141, 3.142).

What constitutes a picture is that its elements are related to one another in a determinate way. (2.14)

Although a picture has names as its constituents it is not a mere

[2] The German text reads, "*Wir machen uns Bilder der Tatsachen*", which rendered literally into English says: "We *make* to ourselves pictures of facts" (Author's italics).

[3] Or, "The elements of the picture represent in the picture the objects".

[4] This makes it clear that elementary propositions are at least among the *class* of pictures, regardless of what else that class may include.

aggregate of names. It has a definite structure which is an *internal* property and hence is intrinsic to it (4.122).[5]

Let us call this connexion of its elements the structure [*Struktur*] of the picture, and let us call the possibility of this structure the pictorial form [*Form der Abbildung*] of the picture. (2.15)

Moreover, the pictorial form (or form of representation) is the necessary condition for the possibility of a picture being a picture *of* reality, or of facts.

What a picture must have in common with reality, in order to be able to depict it — correctly or incorrectly — in the way it does, is its pictorial form. (2.17)

A picture can depict any reality whose form it has. A spatial picture can depict anything spatial, a coloured one anything coloured, etc. (2.171)

The similarity to Kant, at least in the mode of expression, is striking. For Kant, the possibility of knowledge of the world presupposes certain conditions (e.g., the pure forms of understanding and sensibility) in order that our thinking constitute what can validly be called knowledge (*Erkenntnis*) and our experience be of what can validly be called a world. Both these factors are interdependent and their mutual union produces what we call experience (*Erfahrung*). These *a priori* conditions of experience, functioning transcendentally, can be said to constitute the "common element" between thought and reality, which element is *common* because it is "projected" onto our experience (or more exactly, our *Empfindungen*, or pure sensations).[6] Similarly, Witt-

[5] The relations existing between the elements of a class of *aggregates* is, of course, wholly *external*.

[6] Compare the following remarkably Kantian pronouncements. "For the sentence, together with the mode of projection which projects reality into the sentence, determines the logical form of the entities, just as in our simile a picture on plane II, together with its mode of projection, determines the shape of the figure on plane I." Ludwig Wittgenstein, "Some Remarks on Logical Form", *Proceedings of the Aristotelian Society*, Supplement, IX, (1929), p. 169. Here plane I corresponds to the facts or the world, and plane II to the realm of language together with its application. (I do not intend to imply by this parallel with Kant that Wittgenstein is an "idealist" in any usual sense.)

genstein's argument is that if there were nothing in common — identical — between the picture and the fact, i.e., if there were no such thing as pictorial form, we could not picture facts.[7] Indeed, there would then *be* no facts.

Facts are the ultimate "referents" of significant language. We saw in Chapter I that Wittgenstein's grounds for asserting that the world consists of facts and not things is precisely that this is all we can *say*; we can only speak *about* facts. This is related to the *a priori* necessity for the existence of simples, because without them we could not form a picture of the world (2.0211, 2.0212). And just as there must be objects in order for there to be pictures so there must be facts in order for there to be pictures, since a picture is, by definition, a picture *of* a fact (2.12). A "picture" that did not signify a possible fact could neither be true nor false, and would therefore not have a sense (4.063). It would lack its essential character of being a picture — that of being the ultimate unit of meaning — and thus would be no longer a picture. Wittgenstein's doctrine of a common element which is identical in the picture and the fact (together with the theory of names and objects) is, I believe, his answer to the question: What are the necessary conditions for the possibility of significant language? Or, in other words: What is necessary in order that we can speak about — describe — the world at all? His answer is that we can do so because we can form a picture of it, and this shows not only *that* significant language is possible but *how* it is possible.

In 2.15 Wittgenstein defined pictorial form as the *possibility* of the structure of the picture. It is important to see that the common element between language and the world is not its structure (*Struktur*) but its pictorial form. It cannot be structure because the latter is *actual.*

[7] The assertion that there is something common to language and the world does not mean that this "common element" is a *third* thing (*tertium quid*) in addition to language and the facts that somehow exists "between them". Rather, pictorial form is common to both because it is a property of each. Here, the model is not that of analogy, where two things are related by a third, but instead that of (say) two circles, which can be congruent or concentric because they possess the same "shape" or geometrical form.

Its [the state of affair's] form is the possibility of its structure. (2.033)

Meaning, however, is never grounded in or reduced to actuality, but always has reference to the realm of possibilities. Thus, the notion of pictorial form, which expresses this possibility, is designated by Wittgenstein as the common element of pictures and facts. If one keeps the distinction between structure and pictorial form clearly in mind there will be no temptation to make the mistake of grounding meaning in some form of actuality. The latter would be a mistake because it is essential to the picture and its sense to depict a *possible* state of affairs (2.201, 2.202).

But in addition to the pictorial form (*Form der Abbildung*) a picture also has something else in common with reality which enables it to depict it. This is what Wittgenstein calls logical form (*logische Form*).

What any picture, of whatever form, must have in common with reality, in order to be able to depict it — correctly or incorrectly — in any way at all, is logical form, i.e., the form of reality. (2.18)

A picture whose pictorial form is logical form is called a logical picture. (2.181)

Every picture has logical form, but not every picture has (say) spatial or temporal form, though each of the latter has logical form. Further, spatial and temporal forms may also be pictures (have pictorial form). Thus, logical form is not identical with, but embraces, all other kinds of form. The presence of logical form in the picture does not *exclude* that of other forms, but rather enables them to serve their function as pictorial form, i.e., to be possible pictures of the world. It is a necessary *condition* for such a possibility.

Every picture is *at the same time* a logical one. (On the other hand, not every picture is, for example, a spatial one.) (2.182)[8]

[8] Ramsey says the following about the relationship between logical form and pictorial form, based on 2.18 ff. "It appears then, that a picture may have several forms of representation, but one of these must be *the* logical form; and it is not asserted that the picture must have the same logical form as what it pictures, but that all pictures must have *the* logical form." F. P. Ramsey, *The Foundations of Mathematics* (Paterson, New Jersey, Littlefield, Adams & Co.,

So far I have been considering the nature of propositional pictures by themselves, divorced from the reality they represent. But this is a mere expedient of exposition and should not imply that they can be fully understood outside their relationship to facts. This is true for two reasons. First,

A picture is a fact [*Tatsache*]. (2.141)

And second,

The fact that the elements of a picture are related to one another in a determinate way represents that things are related to one another in the same way. (2.15)
Pictorial form is the possibility that things [*Dinge*] are related to one another in the same way as the elements of the picture. (2.151)

In regard to 2.141, we must realize that a picture is a fact only in a restricted sense. A proposition-picture is characterized by an ambiguity similar to that of the type-token ambiguity,[9] namely that between sign and symbol. For Wittgenstein, every proposition is both a sign and a symbol, but the respect in which it is one or the other is quite distinct. Wittgenstein defines a sign as that part of the symbol which is perceptible by the senses (3.32). The symbol may be called the "mode of signification" of the sign (or signs) (3.321). Thus, two or more signs can have the same symbol in common, as in the case of "red" in English and *rot* in German. Also, signs are ultimately arbitrary or conventional, whereas symbols are not (3.322). Ideally, to avoid ambiguity, our language should

1960), p. 272. This distinction between having *the* logical form and having the *same* logical form is a result, I think, of pressing the German text of 2.18 too literally. Wittgenstein does say "*die logische Form*," but the definite article in German does not always carry the notion of uniqueness as it tends to do in English. Wittgenstein's use of it, then, is probably based solely on grammatical convention. I think Ramsey was misled here, and if one reads the passage without undue emphasis on the "*die*" it does say that the picture and the pictured have the *same* logical form.

[9] For the original definitions of "token" and "type" see C. S. Peirce, *Collected Papers*, Vol. IV (Cambridge, Harvard University Press, 1933), pp. 423-424. (I am not claiming that Wittgenstein's discussion follows Peirce's exactly.)

always have a different sign wherever there is a different symbol, and vice versa. This would avoid the confusion of one symbol with another, and would enable us always clearly to distinguish between the meanings of different symbols.

Ramsey expresses the similarity between the type-token distinction and the sign-symbol distinction as follows.

> But a propositional sign [i.e., a sentence] differs essentially from a word because it is not an object or class of objects, but a fact, 'the fact that its elements, the words, are combined in it in a definite way.'
>
> But a *proposition* is a type whose instances consist of all propositional sign tokens which have in common, not a certain appearance [as in the case of a token], but a certain sense.[10]

Thus, *only* as a *sign* and not as a symbol can the proposition be properly regarded as a fact and hence be treated as such.[11] Also, the proposition must be a fact at least in *some* sense because only a fact can have the isomorphism with another fact which is so crucial to Wittgenstein's theory of meaning. Thus, one fact as a sign pictures another fact by virtue of the isomorphism of pictorial form. This raises the question of why one fact is a picture and another is the fact pictured. I do not think this can be settled *a priori*. It is clear, however, that not *all* facts can function as pictures, because their mere physical or perceptible properties (which make them signs) may not be sufficient to make them also pictures, i.e., to give them pictorial form. A picture, in addition to being a sign, is also a symbol, and a picture's *being* a symbol is largely determined by its function as a part of our language (3.326, 3.327, 3.328). That is, a fact becomes a picture-symbol by acquiring a specific *role* in language. This acquisition is, I think, ultimately based on such non-philosophical considerations as need, purpose and practicability. But it must be remembered that

[10] Ramsey, *op. cit.*, p. 274.

[11] My reasons for asserting this will be given in Chapter IV when I discuss Wittgenstein's mysticism . It is one of the basic theses of my whole interpretation of the *Tractatus* (as opposed to that of the positivists) that the distinction between sign and symbol both makes possible, and to a large extent constitutes, Wittgenstein's mysticism.

a necessary *condition* for a fact becoming a picture-symbol is that it, by virtue of its *also* being a sign, possess the same logical form as the fact which it is intended to depict.

"A picture is a fact, the fact that its elements are combined with one another in a definite way."[12] This brings us to 2.15 (quoted above), where Wittgenstein says that the fact *that* the elements of the picture are related in a certain way "represents" that the objects in the fact are so related. 2.151 asserts in addition that the possibility of representing this coordination of the elements of picture and fact is the pictorial form of the proposition. Indeed, this coordination is what makes a picture a picture — it is what renders a fact a *proposition*-fact, or sign.

We saw earlier that the elementary proposition is essentially a "concatenation" of names. The names designate the simple objects in the fact. This is now seen as an essential characteristic of the proposition as a *picture*, for what the proposition-picture does when it pictures facts is to represent that the objects in the fact are coordinated with the names in the proposition (2.15).

> Thus there are two distinct features belonging to a picture ...: first, the relation between the elements of the picture; and second, the correlations of the elements in the picture with things outside the picture... .[13]

This correlation of the elements of the picture and the fact is *external* in that the relations of the elements of the picture are significant before the correlation, and *internal* in that the elements actually do have a congruity of structure.[14] The external correlation is thus a result of the practical application of propositions to reality, whereas the internal relation is the necessary condition for this application, and hence is logical.

In every picture, therefore, the names must have (1) the same *order* and (2) the same *multiplicity* as the objects in the fact pictured.

[12] Ramsey, *op. cit.*, p. 271.

[13] G. E. M. Anscombe, *An Introduction to Wittgenstein's Tractatus* (London, Hutchinson University Library, 1959), p. 68.

[14] *Ibid.*, p. 67.

In a proposition there must be exactly as many distinguishable parts as in the situation [*Sachlage*] that it represents.

The two must possess the same logical (mathematical) multiplicity. (4.04)[15]

Let us consider the following passage, which is intended to be an illustration of the above.

We must not say "The complex sign '*aRb*' says '*a* stands in relation *R* to *b*'"; but we must say, "that 'a' stands in a certain relation to '*b*' says that *aRb*". (3. 1432)

The above has been a constant source of perplexity and misunderstanding to commentators and critics of the *Tractatus*, and has led to a great deal of confusion and error. In fact, many critics cite it as proving the very opposite of what I maintain it proves. I hold that it shows that there is an exact one-to-one correspondence between picture and fact in regard to order and multiplicity (at least for relational statements of two or more places). However, critics have taken this passage to show that in at least this class of statements (i.e., relational statements) the necessary one-to-one correspondence breaks down, and that the isomorphism of order and multiplicity between picture and fact is either impossible or nonexistent. Such a view is strongly argued for by Daitz, Stenius, and Evans.[16] Now, *if* such criticisms are valid we must conclude that there are serious and perhaps insuperable difficulties at the very heart of Wittgenstein's picture theory of meaning. I therefore think that it is necessary to discuss them in detail and try to give

[15] Wittgenstein asserts this necessity in terms of the concept of number when he says that when we analyze the logical structure of facts we must use *numbers* in our elementary propositions. Moreover, this is not just a special feature of our symbolism. Cite "Some Remarks on Logical Form", *op. cit.*, pp. 165-166.

[16] Edna Daitz, "The Picture Theory of Meaning", in *Essays in Conceptual Analysis*, ed. by Antony Flew (London, MacMillan & Co. Ltd., 1960). Erik Stenius, *Wittgenstein's Tractatus: A Critical Exposition of Its Main Lines of Thought* (Oxford, Basil Blackwell, 1960). Ellis Evans, "*Tractatus* 3.1432", *Mind*, LXIV, No. 254 (April 1955), pp. 259-260; and "About 'aRb'", *Mind*, LXVIII, No. 272 (October 1959), pp. 535-538.

an adequate reply. The criticisms are all basically concerned with the question of *multiplicity*. That is, they deny Wittgenstein's assertion that for every element in the picture there is a corresponding element in the fact, and vice versa. I will begin with Daitz, whose basic objection, assuming the picture theory to be true and applicable to ordinary language, is that "... all ordinary sentences have, for fact-stating purposes, one word too many!"

As an example in ordinary language of a sentence of the form "aRb" Daitz takes the sentence "Sophia hates Amos". Her point is that there is one *more* element in the sentence "Sophia hates Amos" than there is in the fact that *Sophia hates Amos*, and in general, that every sentence of this form will have n + 1 elements in the sentence for n elements in the fact.

For the sentence is the fact '*Hates*' *is between* '*Sophia*' *and* '*Amos*', *i.e.* it has four elements while *Sophia hates Amos* has only three.[17]

This criticism completely misses the point of what Wittgenstein is saying in 3.1432, and also shows that Daitz fails to understand what Wittgenstein meant in 2.03 when he said: "In a state of affairs objects fit into one another like the links of a chain". First, Daitz fails to see the *point* of the chain metaphor. In a chain, one link x is directly connected to another link y; there is no "third" link *between* x and y which connects them to each other. Nor is this necessary. The linkage of a chain is not a "thing" as the links themselves are; *that* two links are connected together *shows* itself.[18] Second, as regards 3.1432, Wittgenstein is really saying that "R" in "aRb" is not a *name*, and that the *R* in the fact *aRb* is not an *object*; relations are not things and should not be treated as such. This is the real import of the chain metaphor in 2.03. Thus, in an ideal notation the "R" in the sentence "aRb" would not appear, precisely because it is not essential to the picturing of the fact. For instance, if "a" and "b" designated spatial objects the spatial arrangement of the elements of the sign would picture

[17] Daitz, *op. cit.*, p. 59.

[18] See Anscombe, *op. cit.*, p. 36 ff.

the spatial arrangement of the objects in the fact. That is, "a" being to the left of "b" in the sign "ab" would *show* that *a* is to the left of *b* in the fact *ab*, or vice versa, if the relation is "to the right of". Hence, the spatial order would *show* what the ultimately superfluous sign "R" misleadingly tries to *say* (Cf. 3.1431). Therefore, instead of there being *four* elements in the picture and three in the fact, as Daitz contends, there are really only *two* in each, and the structural homogeneity of picture and fact is not lost.

The above is crucial for an understanding of Wittgenstein's logical doctrine of the independence of elementary propositions and his corresponding ontological doctrine of pluralism. One of the classic philosophical arguments against pluralism, from Plato's *Parmenides*[19] to Bradley, is the attempt to show that the assertion of the reality of relations (both spatial and temporal) leads to an infinite regress, thus apparently proving the truth of monism. This argument is based on the treatment of relations as "objects" or terms, hence being things which *themselves* have to be related. Thus, if R relates x and y, and, *ex hypothesi*, R itself is a term, we must posit R_1 to relate R to x and y, and R_2 to relate R_1 to R and x and y, *ad infinitum*. This is precisely what Daitz has done when she says that the sentence-fact "Sophia hates Amos" has four elements, namely, "Sophia", "hates", "Amos", and "hates-being-between-Sophia-and-Amos", although she does not draw the consequence of the infinite regress.[20]

The above position is exactly what Wittgenstein is intent on escaping from, and Daitz's argument completely begs the question because of her failure to see this. For Wittgenstein (as we have seen in Chapter II) relations and properties are not objects (*Gegenstände*), and relation-signs are not names. There are no "logical objects", and the logical constants, –, V, &, etc., are *operations*, not *constituents* of the picture-proposition. When Wittgenstein says that objects are connected like links in a chain he means that

[19] See Plato, *Parmenides*, in *The Dialogues of Plato*, trans. by B. Jowett, Vol. II (New York, Random House, 1937), 132 ff.

[20] Daitz, *op. cit.*, p. 59.

two objects can be related without presupposing another relation to relate the first two, and so on.

The mode of union of two substances (and 'objects make up the substance of the world' in 2.021) is not another substance coming between them and therefore separating rather than connecting them. Their relation is simply their mode of union, their connection.[21]

This can also be seen from the following consideration. If "R" in "aRb" could be taken as a *term* then one could write $(R_2(R_1(a,b)))$, that is, allow R to be an argument of *itself*. (This is what Daitz and the infinite regress argument both assume.) But it is essential for Wittgenstein that a function cannot be its own argument, i.e., "R_2" cannot fill the blank in the function $(\#(R_1(a,b)))$. This is the basis of Wittgenstein's rejection of Russell's theory of types and the possibility of a hierarchy of meta-languages, and ultimately, his mysticism (Cf. 3.332 ff.), which will be discussed in detail in the next chapter.

Here, I think, is the appropriate place to clarify a similar confusion about the same problem. I am referring to Evans' "refutation" of Daitz's "refutation", in which he claims that Daitz is wrong in saying that there is one *more* element in the picture than in the fact because (according to him) there is an additional element in the *fact* also. Now, in trying to correct Daitz, Evans falls into a different though analogous error. Thus, where Daitz says that the fourth element in the picture is the relation holding between the three terms, "Sophia", "hates", and "Amos", Evans says there is also a fourth element in the *fact*, namely, the relation (the "grouping") holding between Sophia, hates and Amos. It is this relation of "grouping" which corresponds to the fourth element in the picture, thereby preserving the homogeneity of structure of picture and fact. Thus, the picture-fact ratio for Daitz is 4:3, and for Evans 4:4.

Wittgenstein says that we must not take the *complex sign* as saying that *a* stands in R to *b*. I take this as meaning that we must not say that the

[21] I. M. Copi, Review of Stenius' *Wittgenstein's Tractatus, A Critical Exposition of Its Main Lines of Thought*, in *Philosophical Review*, LXXII, No. 3, p. 386.

group says that, but that the *grouping* says that, the way the elements of the complex sign are ordered.

Wittgenstein would have said, I think, that the fact that Sophia hates Amos contained four elements: the two peoples, the hating, and the structure of these... .[22]

I think that one can see that Evans is wrong for the same reasons as Daitz, and that the arguments I used against the latter would also apply, *mutatis mutandis*, to him. The isomorphism of picture and fact cannot be retained in this way. In trying to prevent Wittgenstein from making one error he forces him into another analogous one.

Finally, I would like to call attention to similar errors made by Stenius on this same point. His mistakes arise chiefly from his opinion that properties and relations, as well as what he calls "individual things", are included among Wittgensteins objects. (My opposition to this view was argued in detail in Chapter II). Thus, Stenius' account, like Daitz's and Evans', is based on the treatment of relations as objects (*Gegenstände*). To argue his point he takes the sentence, "The moon is smaller than the earth", which he analyzes into, "mSe", i.e., into a statement designating two individual things joined by a dyadic relation.[23] Stenius gives two interpretations of this sentence in terms of the picture theory. The first (1) he calls the "false key" of interpretation, and the second (2) he calls the "true key" of interpretation.[24] The argument is as follows. (1) The sentence "mSe" as a sign is a fact consisting of *three* elements, each of which is a name: "m", "e", and "S".[25] First, he points out that the strict isomorphism of picture and fact is broken, because in the sentence "S" is an object whereas in the fact *s* is a relation.[26] Second, the sentence-fact "mSe" has *four* elements:

[22] Evans, *op. cit.*, p. 260.
[23] Stenius, *op. cit.*, p. 130.
[24] *Ibid.*, p. 132.
[25] *Ibid.*, p. 130.
[26] Stenius' terminology is confusing here. Calling the sign "S" an "object" is odd, and distinguishing it from the S in the fact on this basis seems unjustifiable, since he classifies relations as objects also.

"m", "S", "e" (all of which are again names), and what he calls the "triadic concatenation relation", which is

... The relation that holds between three objects, when the first is immediately to the left of the second and the second is immediately to the left of the third.

And then it cannot be isomorphic with the fact that the moon is smaller than the earth, because this fact is analyzed into three elements only.[27]

(2) In his second interpretation Stenius asserts that the isomorphism of picture and fact in "mSe" can be maintained if we deny that "S" is an *object* in the sentence-fact. Instead, we "... must regard it only as a *characteristic* of a dyadic relation... ."[28] (That is, we must no longer regard the relation-sign "S" as an "object".) The three elements of the sentence-fact are thus: the name "m", the name "e", and the relation-character "S". (1) then is the "false key" of interpretation for it asserts that there is one more element in the picture than there is in the fact (Daitz's position); and (2) is the "true key" because it preserves the necessary isomorphism of picture and fact.

Stenius' analysis is, I think, tortured. The identification of relations with objects is at the basis of the trouble. And since, as I have argued, Wittgenstein did not make this identification, there are no grounds for distinguishing between a true and a false key of interpretation and asserting that Wittgenstein vacillated between them. In fact, *both* of Stenius' interpretations are wrong. (1) he rejects himself as incompatible with the picture theory. In (2) he concludes that there is a three-three correspondence between picture and fact. This too is mistaken because for Wittgenstein relations are neither objects nor "individual things." The isomorphism of "mSe" to *mSe* is hence two to two, just as that of "aRb" to *aRb* (above).

Having concluded this analysis I think it is the proper place to mention what I believe to be further misunderstandings of Wittgenstein's picture theory of meaning, and attempt to give a

[27] Stenius, *op. cit.*, p. 131.

[28] *Ibid.*, p. 131. It is hard to understand what Stenius means by calling "S" a "characteristic" of a dyadic relation.

satisfactory reply to them. While this discussion will be basically polemical in nature I believe that it will, in addition to defending the picture theory, also serve further to clarify some of its essential features. I will concern myself primarily with Daitz since I think that her views are representative of many of the commonest mistakes about the picture theory.

Daitz opens her article by giving the following definition of the picture theory of meaning, which she intends to apply to Wittgenstein's *Tractatus*.

> How can words have meaning? You may answer that a word is, in a way, a picture, and that its meaning is what it pictures; and if words are put together to make a sentence, they can picture a more complex unit, the fact. Let us call this the Picture Theory of Meaning. I hope to show why it must be a wrong account of 'how words mean.'[29]

Now, the first thing that should be said is that Daitz's definition of the picture theory of meaning does *not* apply to Wittgenstein at all. For Daitz, the picture theory is intended to show how *words* have meaning, which meaning she says consists in their being "pictures" of something else. This view implies that the word (as opposed to the sentence or proposition) is the basic unit of meaning (*Sinn*).[30] Both these assertions are completely false as regards the *Tractatus* and foreign to the whole argument of the book. In the *Tractatus* Wittgenstein is primarily concerned with how a *proposition* (which is not, moreover, a mere group of words (3.141)) can have meaning, not its constituents. The proposition, then, not the word, is the ultimate unit of meaning or sense. Also, Wittgenstein says explicitly in several places that words, or names, do *not* have meaning (*Sinn*) (Cite 3.142, 3.144, 3.203, 3.3). That the name is not the basic unit of meaning can be seen from 3.3, where Wittgenstein says that:

[29] Daitz, *op. cit.*, p. 53.

[30] When Daitz talks about meaning she does not distinguish between *Sinn* and *Bedeutung*. But her account of the picture theory, in which words are pictures, *implies* that words (or names) have *Sinn*. This is why she is wrong about the *Tractatus*. If she had said that words only have *Bedeutung* she would have been relatively safe, but of course then she could not talk about *pictures*, for a picture is a picture in virtue of its *Sinn*.

Only propositions have sense [*Sinn*]; only in the nexus of a proposition does a name have meaning [*Bedeutung*]. (3.3)

Thus, a "name" by itself is not really a name, for it can only perform its essential function, i.e., naming, by first entering into the "nexus" or context of a proposition. Therefore, when Daitz says, "The ideal name would picture, say, a particular",[31] it is clear that this view is totally foreign to the *Tractatus*.

If a slight digression may be permitted, I would like to suggest a possible *source* of Daitz's misunderstanding of Wittgenstein's views on this crucial point. Perhaps she was thinking of his remarks in §46 of the *Philosophical Investigations*[32] where he refers to Plato's *Theatetus*. In §46 ff. Wittgenstein is concerned with criticizing certain views, primarily the theory of simples (objects) put forward in the *Tractatus*. In the selection from the *Theatetus* which he quotes the theory discussed is one in which words (names) are asserted as the basic units of meaning, individual perceptible objects being their referrents.[33] Although there are analogues between the view in the *Theatetus* and the *Tractatus* there are also crucial differences. And it is the differences which are to the point here, namely, that in the *Tractatus* the proposition, *not names*, is the ultimate unit of meaning or sense (*Sinn*). In other words, Daitz is (wrongly) ascribing to Wittgenstein in the *Tractatus* the theory (or part of it) expressed in the *Theatetus*.

Daitz's whole argument reduces to a criticism of the notion of a picture used as a *model* for *all* language, especially ordinary language. This model, she feels, does not adequately describe the way language has meaning, and indeed, often distorts it. For instance, Daitz classifies all pictures, together with reflections and maps, as *icons*, an icon being "... a sign which has at least one of the properties of that which it is a sign, and signifies in virtue of such a property".[34] Language, she says, is not iconic because it

[31] Daitz, *op. cit.*, p. 71.

[32] Ludwig Wittgenstein, *Philosophical Investigations*, trans. by G. E. M. Anscombe (New York, MacMillan Co., 1953).

[33] Plato, *Theatetus*, in *The Dialogues of Plato*, Vol. II, trans. by B. Jowett (New York, Random House, 1937), 201c ff.

[34] Daitz, *op. cit.*, p. 59.

signifies "conventionally", whereas an icon signifies "essentially". Thus, the demand that language signify in the same way as icons results in a misdescription of language.[35] Daitz does not explain this distinction between conventional and essential signification, however. Indeed, the blank assertion that language signifies conventionally raises suspicions that she is begging the whole question, for one of the main purposes of the *Tractatus* is to show *how* the conventional aspects of language (e.g., signs) *can* signify, and the answer given is that this is possible only because there is something *non*-conventional about language (Cf. 2.16 ff.). This is the whole *point* of the picture theory of meaning!

What Daitz is trying to say here, I think, is that a thing can signify, represent, or picture another thing only if it is *like* it, just as an icon is "like" its original. Now first, it should be pointed out that Wittgenstein never uses the term "icon", and does not demand that a linguistic picture be "like" the thing it signifies the way an icon is. This can be seen from 4.002, where he says that the "outward form" of language (i.e., ordinary language) is so *un*like the "form of the thought beneath it" (i.e., its logical form) that we cannot "infer" the latter from the former. Also, in his essay, "Some Remarks on Logical Form"[36] Wittgenstein distinguishes between that which is to be projected (the source) and the *method* of projection. Due to the latter, that which is projected (the result) is radically *un*like the source, while the relation of "picturing" is not destroyed. In fact, Wittgenstein held that this is, for the most part, what actually happens in the case of ordinary language. In addition, the proposition-picture and what is pictured (the fact) need not be of the same *kind*. For instance, a spatial relation in the sign can picture a temporal relation in the fact, as when musical notes in the printed score are arranged spatially, but when played or sung are temporal. The score, nevertheless, remains a picture of the music as it is actually performed. Also,

[35] *Ibid.*, p. 67.

[36] Ludwig Wittgenstein, "Some Remarks on logical Form", *Proceedings of the Aristotelian Society*, Supplement, IX (1929), pp. 162-171. (Cite pp. 164-165 esp.).

a dark color in a painting (e.g., a landscape) can represent spatial distance, as when the foreground is dominated by light colors and the background by shaded ones.[37]

Daitz makes two other assertions which are also irrelevant to the *Tractatus*, although they are intended to be relevant. The first is:

Since the elements of a sentence do not represent elements in the signified, *a fortiori*, the elements of a sentence do not correspond to elements in the signified.[38]

But, as has already been pointed out, Wittgenstein does not maintain that the elements of a sentence (i.e., the words) "represent", and hence does not base the correspondence of sentence-elements with fact-elements on this. Second, Daitz asks:

Why are negative statements, conditional statements, disjunctive statements, etc. not describable in picture terms? The reason is that they are the very statements which have no pictorial counter-parts.[39]

This criticism rests on a gross misunderstanding. It is again wholly irrelevant to the *Tractatus* because Wittgenstein does not hold that complex propositions picture in themselves or that the logical constants, "-", "V", "&", etc., are elements or constituents of the picture. Only elementary propositions can strictly be said to picture facts.[40] Complex propositions "picture" only in so far as their elementary constituents do. This is possible because of the truth-functional nature of propositions and because the logical constants are not names. In this same connection Daitz asks how we can form a picture of the fact that (say) a cat *will* be on the mat, or *was* on the mat.[41] This too is beside the point, for it is the essence of the proposition that it pictures what *is* the case. A proposition pictures future and past facts by asserting what *is* the case; differences in grammatical tense do not affect this function. Daitz

[37] I. M. Copi, "Objects, Properties and Relations in the *Tractatus*", *Mind*, LXVII, No. 266 (April 1958), p. 157.

[38] Daitz, *op. cit.*, p. 64.

[39] *Ibid.*, p. 68.

[40] Cf. Copi, *op. cit.*, p. 148 ff. (See also Chapter VI of this book).

[41] Daitz, *op. cit.*, p. 69.

confuses a logical property with a conventional grammatical one. I form a picture of the fact that a cat *will* be on the mat by asserting a proposition which says what *is* the case *if* it is true. And this is what every proposition does.

In concluding this section of her argument Daitz asserts a mistaken equation between the theory of language in the *Tractatus* and that suggested in Plato's *Cratylus*.

Thus we might say that 'the name like the picture is an imitation of the thing' (Plato, *Cratylus* 430) or that 'The proposition is a picture of reality' (*Tractatus* 4.12).[42]

Without going into a detailed discussion of the *Cratylus* I think it is sufficient to point out that the theory of language proposed there is based on a distinction between a "real" language, a language which exists "by nature", and a conventional one. The mark of the former is that its words would bear a literal resemblance to the things they signify. (For instance, a person named "Dolores" would actually be of a melancholy temperament, or a person who is short in height would have a correspondingly short name, like "Ed".) Now it is clear that such a literal resemblance is not in question at all in the *Tractatus*, for the picture does not have to be "like" the pictured. Daitz's equation of the latter with the theory in the *Cratylus* is thus irrelevant.

I have now concluded my discussion of the picture theory of meaning in so far as it is related to the nature of elementary propositions. The basic thought I have tried to express is that the notion of pictorial form and the isomorphism of picture and fact lie at the heart of Wittgenstein's theory. The essence of the picture theory may be summarized, I think, in the following way. In order for language to describe the world (i.e., in order for there to be propositions) it is necessary to presuppose a common form between picture and fact. This common form (conceived of as a necessary condition, not an actuality) is what Wittgenstein calls logical form. *Thus, it is because, and only because, both language and the world possess a common logical structure that it is possible*

[42] *Ibid.*, p. 70.

for the one to describe the other. Such description is called picturing — language picture, mirrors, or reflects the world. Pictorial form may therefore be called the necessary presupposition for the possibility of meaning, the latter of course being understood as cognitive, and not (say) emotive meaning.[43]

Having seen that pictorial form constitutes the *possibility* of a common form (or isomorphism) between language and the world we found that there are at least two necessary conditions for the *actualization* of the picturing relation. These are order and multiplicity, which taken together define this isomorphism. At this point it was necessary to turn to a critique of some of the commonest misinterpretations of the picture theory of meaning. The most important conclusions reached were the following. (1) Relations are not objects (or terms) and therefore relational sentences like "aRb" can possess the required isomorphism with their respective facts. (A corollary to this is that Wittgenstein's theory of relations avoids the danger of the infinite regress argument traditionally urged against pluralism.) (2) The picture theory is intended to explain how sentences (i.e., elementary propositions) have meaning, and not words. (3) The picture does not have to be *like* the fact except in *form* — pictures are not icons — and hence the relationship of logical pictures to ordinary language cannot be undermined by pointing out their *apparent* discrepancy. And (4) it was found that complex propositions, *qua* complex, are not pictures.

Having discovered in this chapter that pictorial form is the essential characteristic of propositions as pictures it is necessary to turn to Wittgenstein's mysticism, as the latter is a direct logical consequence of this very notion. Indeed, I believe that without a full comprehension of Wittgenstein's mysticism an understanding of pictorial form, and hence of the theory of meaning in general, is not possible. I will therefore conclude my exposition of meaning with a discussion of the nature of mysticism (*das Mystische*).

[43] In Chapter VI it will be seen that pictorial form is also a necessary condition for the possibility of *truth*, the latter being conceived as the *actual* agreement of the picture with the fact.

IV

MEANING, LOGICAL FORM, AND MYSTICISM

> There are, indeed, things that cannot be put into words. They *make themselves manifest*. They are what is mystical. (6. 522)

This chapter concludes my treatment of meaning. It is an attempt to give a coherent exposition of Wittgenstein's mysticism (*das Mystische*) in relation to theory of meaning and logical form, at least to the extent to which this is possible. I add the latter qualification because in the case of *das Mystische* the very nature of the subject delimits to some extent what and how much can actually be said about it. (This will become clearer later on.) But regardless of the problem inherent in saying what Wittgenstein's mysticism *is* it is still possible to show its *relationship* to the rest of his thought. This is essentially what I wish to do in the following pages. That is, I wish to show that the mystical is an essential characteristic of the philosophical views of the *Tractatus*, and that it is a direct and necessary consequence of the theory of meaning expounded in it. More exactly, I hope to show how the mystical is a direct consequence of Wittgenstein's concept of logical form, which itself lies at the heart of the picture theory.

In the course of this chapter the following problems will be discussed. First, I will state briefly some of the most important characteristics of Wittgenstein's conception of the nature and function of logical analysis, particularly in regard to ordinary language. The conclusions of these remarks will lead into a discussion of pictorial and logical form, the latter being seen now as the ultimate foundations of the mystical consequences of Wittgenstein's theory of meaning. At this point the crucial distinction between saying (*sagen*) and showing (*zeigen*) will emerge, and will become the focus of my further treatment of the mystical. In other words, I will try to bring out the relationship of showing and mysticism (in so far as theory of meaning is concerned) by illustrating how the latter is a necessary consequence of the former, which in turn grows out of the notion of logical form. The next section will be mainly critical, in that I will take up one of the most important attempts — that of Carnap — to avert the necessity of mysticism by denying the doctrine of showing. Here I will deal with Carnap's view that the logical form of language can be articulated by means of the formal mode-material mode distinction, which distinction purportedly enables one to express in another language what cannot be said in that language itself. Having sketched the main outlines of Carnap's position I will contrast it to Wittgenstein's and show why the latter cannot accept it. This will be done by means of a discussion of the infinite regress argument as related to the language hierarchy. Due to the distinction between a benign and a vicious infinite regress it will be seen that Wittgenstein's position is ultimately and radically incompatible with that represented by Carnap, and cannot be modified in terms of it. The traditional "third Man" argument in Plato's *Parmenides* will be recalled and related to the problem that Wittgenstein is concerned with in the *Tractatus.* In conclusion, I will make a brief allusion to Wittgenstein's "solution" of the so-called problem of the relationship between thought (or language) and reality.

Wittgenstein's use of the term "*das Mystische*" may be unfortunate, in that it is notoriously vague in itself, and also has many connotations and associations which are quite foreign to its meaning in the context of the *Tractatus.*[1] Curiously enough, "*das Mystische*" appears in only three places in the *Tractatus*, at 6.44, 6.45, and 6.522. This is ironical considering the amount that has been said about it and the bewilderment and even shock it has caused in some circles. However, despite the quantitative infrequency of its use I believe that mysticism is one of the most significant and crucial aspects of Wittgenstein's early thought, and is of

[1] This may be especially true in the case of German. "*Mystisch*" is an adjectival form derived from the noun "*Mysterium*", which means "mystery".

profound philosophical importance. It also has been argued that "*das Mystische*" is used by Wittgenstein in more than one *sense*.[2] Although this opinion is true to a certain extent I think that ultimately one can see that "*das Mystische*" has a single root meaning. What is misleading is that the notion of mysticism can be approached and seen from several different points of view. Once these points of view are contemplated together, however, one realizes that they all converge on one central idea. This central idea, or root meaning is, I believe, the notion of the world (*die Welt*) as a limited whole (*als begrenztes Ganzes*).

Feeling the world as a limited whole — it is this that is mystical. (6.45)

Given this radical finitude one "feels" (*fühlt*) that something lies "outside" the world. (Of course, this "outsideness" should not be thought of in simply spatial terms.) Wittgenstein includes among the latter God (6.432), the "solution of the riddle [*des Rätsels*] of life" (6.4312), the sense (*Sinn*) of the world, and value (*Wert*) (6.41). But the condition that is necessary for these things to lie *beyond* the world of *Sachverhalte* is that the latter be radically finite, or in other words, be a *limited* whole. This finitude reveals itself in several ways. One way is that the *Elementarsätze* can state only facts and not value (*Wert*) (6.42). Another way, and one more important for our present purposes, is that the logical form of language itself cannot be expressed (*gesagt*) *by* language.

Propositions can represent the whole of reality, but they cannot represent what they must have in common with reality in order to be able to represent it — logical form. (4.12)

What expresses *itself* in language, *we* cannot express by means of language. (4.121)

In other words, the world is limited in that some things cannot be *said*; our language and thought are characterized by an intrinsic and essential finitude. Thus, given the basic connection between the world as a limited whole and *das Mystische*, the latter in turn is seen to be related to theory of meaning via logical form and "what

[2] Frank R. Harrison, "Notes on Wittgenstein's Use of '*das Mystische*'", *The Southern Journal of Philosophy*, I, No. 3 (Fall, 1963), pp. 3-9.

cannot be expressed". In this chapter, therefore, I am concerned with this one aspect of *das Mystische*, namely, its relation to meaning in general and logical form in particular.

I have stated that it is the main purpose of this chapter to show how Wittgenstein's mysticism is an intrinsic characteristic of his theory of meaning and even a direct consequence of it. More specifically, it is my contention that to attempt to retain the picture theory while rejecting the element of mysticism is impossible. At worst it results in self-contradiction, and at best one would arrive at a theory which, regardless of its own merits, would certainly not be Wittgenstein's. In my own study of the *Tractatus* I have found a peculiar tendency among critics and commentators[3] to systematically disregard the *seriousness* with which Wittgenstein asserted his position on this matter. I must now try to justify my own contention that *das Mystische* is crucial to Wittgenstein's theory of meaning, despite the *prima facie* appearance to the contrary. This in effect constitutes the main argument of this chapter.

We saw earlier (Chapter III) that pictorial form and logical form constitute the common element between the picture and the fact, or more precisely, between the picture-fact (the sign) and the fact pictured. Also, we saw that this isomorphism is internal to both picture and fact, and hence it is impossible that they not possess it (4.14, 4.1221, 4.123). The propositional sign, then, must have a common structure with the fact *if* it is to picture it. When this condition is met[4] the proposition-sign can become a *symbol* and function as a genuine proposition, that is, as a picture of the world. This brings us to a consideration of the nature of logical or philosophical analysis.

[3] I include in this class even such an eminent thinker as Ramsey, who, despite his intimacy and sympathetic understanding of much of Wittgenstein's early thought, seemed unwilling or unable to come to terms with his mysticism. F. P. Ramsey, *The Foundations of Mathematics* (Paterson, New Yersey, Littlefield, Adams & Co., 1960), pp. 285-286. Russell's attitude on this question is similar. (Cf. p. xxi of his Introduction to the *Tractatus*).

[4] This in itself is a necessary condition but not a sufficient one. An additional requirement is that there be *users* of language who are able to apply the proposition-signs to reality.

For Wittgenstein, it is the business of logical analysis to uncover the real form of the proposition-sign so that the structure of the fact becomes manifest. In ordinary language the sign "disguises" or obscures the real form of the sign and hence of the fact. Generally, Wittgenstein's doctrine of language in the *Tractatus* is not (as Russell thought)[5] an attempt to construct an *ideal* symbolism above and beyond ordinary language, such that the latter must either conform to it or be cast away as ambiguous and unfit for scientific purposes. Nor is it an attempt to *reform* ordinary language.

In fact, all the propositions of our everyday language, just as they stand, are in perfect logical order. (5.5563)

Rather, logical analysis tries to find the logical form which is *already* there. After all, we *do* picture the world, and we *do* assert propositions without knowing beforehand if they are true. We do not have to study the *Principia Mathematica* or formulate an "ideal" language in order to talk meaningfully about the world. As we have seen, elementary propositions are a logical necessity for significant discourse. Moreover, they are inherent *in* our language precisely *because* of this *a priori* necessity.

If we know on purely logical grounds that there must be elementary propositions, then everyone who understands propositions in their unanalyzed form must know it. (5.5562)

This does not imply, however, that we can merely look at language and "see" that it consists of *Elementarsätze*. Meaning for Wittgenstein is never something actual that we can find by "looking around" and seeing it there staring us in the face, nor is it a "property" of propositions or words. The actual grammatical structure of the sentences of ordinary language obscures its logical structure, but this structure is nonetheless always present. (Cf. also 5.5563). But because of this obscuration

It is not humanly possible to gather immediately from it what the logic of language is.

[5] Cf. Russell's Introduction to the *Tractatus*, p. x.

Everyday language is a part of the human organism and is no less complicated than it. (4.002)[6]

Why is ordinary language so "complicated", and why is it impossible simply to *infer* its underlying logic by looking at it? The explanation, I think, lies in Wittgenstein's concept of the method of projection of propositions (Cf. Chapter III), and of the proposition in its projective relation to the world (3.11 ff.). Wittgenstein does not say much about this in the *Tractatus*, but he does give a very interesting and helpful illustration of it in the later essay, "Some Remarks on Logical Form". There he uses a metaphor consisting of two planes, on one of which are inscribed geometrical figures, and a method of projecting the images of one plane onto the other by means of a *rule* of projection.

If we decide to project *different* images from Plane I to II (e.g., to a circle in I corresponds a square on II) we can't tell by looking at II what it corresponds to on I. We need to know both the particular figure in I and the particular rule of projection used.

These forms are the norms of our particular language into which we project in *ever so many* ways *ever so many* different logical forms. And for this very reason we can draw no conclusions — except very vague ones — from the use of these norms as to the actual logical form of the phenomena described.

In this way, Wittgenstein concludes,

... We find logical forms which have very little similarity with the norms of ordinary language.[7]

[6] I wish to add parenthetically that I do not believe, contrary to conventional opinion, that Wittgenstein wholly rejected this view in the *Philosophical Investigations*. The appeal there also is never to the *actual* language spoken by the man-on-the-street in Oxford, England, in the second quarter of the 20th century, as this is defined by the *O. E. D.* In the *Philosophical Investigations* the appeal is always to the *possible* — hence the *construction* of language games. This is why many of Wittgenstein's self-styled "disciples" have really distorted his views by their constant reference to what people *actually* say. The consequence is that they may be doing "sociological linguistics" but not philosophy.

[7] Ludwig Wittgenstein, "Some Remarks on Logical Form", *Proceedings of the Aristotelian Society*, Supplement, IX (1929), pp. 164-165.

But it must be remembered that the difficulties involved in *finding* the basic logical structure of ordinary language do not imply that such a structure is not present.

The above gives us the germ of Wittgenstein's concepts of logic, logical analysis, and philosophy, as well as the key to his mysticism. For Wittgenstein, logic is not a *science*. It does not have a "subject matter" peculiar to itself, e.g., so-called "logical objects" or the "laws of thought". It is thus not a "theory" about the world, or about something *in* the world. Rather, it is an activity which sets the *limits* to the world, "mirroring" the logical properties of significant propositions, tautologies, and contradictions (5.16, 6.13).[8] Further, these "logical properties" cannot themselves constitute the subject-matter of a theory, or of philosophy. That is why they can only be "mirrored". (Cf. 4.12 and 4.121 below). Since logic is not a theory it is also not a *system* and cannot be identified with any given symbolic formulation, like the *Principia Mathematica.* (Thus, there can be no "plurality" of logics.)[9] Rather, logic is concerned with what is *common* to all such systems. This common element cannot be explicitly expressed, for any attempt to do so presupposes it. Instead, it *shows* (*zeigt*) itself in terms of the signs and rules used to manipulate the symbols. Russell could think of an "ideal" language to which all other languages must approximate only because he thought of logic as a system, and in particular, as identical with the system of the *Principia.* In short, logical analysis, or philosophy, aims at revealing the logic of language and the world by *displaying* (*darstellen*) the pictorial form of propositions. And since pictorial form cannot be expressed (*gesagt*) (4.12) philosophy is an *activity*, not a *theory* or body of doctrine (4.111, 4.112).

We are now in a position to see the point from which Wittgenstein's mysticism emerges. This is the notion of logical form (*logische Form*).

[8] Alexander P. Maslow, *A Study of Ludwig Wittgenstein's Tractatus Logico-Philosophicus* (Berkeley, Cal., University of California Press, 1961), p. 51 ff.
[9] *Ibid.*, pp. 58-59.

Propositions [*Der Satz*] can represent [*darstellen*] the whole of reality, but they cannot represent what they must have in common with reality in order to represent it — the logical form [*logische Form*]. (4.12)

Propositions cannot represent logical form; it is mirrored [*spiegelt sich*] in them.

What finds its reflection in language, language cannot represent.

What expresses *itself* in language, *we* cannot express by means of language. (4.121)

The second half of 4.12 above reads,

In order to be able to represent logical form, we should have to be able to station ourselves with propositions somewhere outside logic, that is to say outside the world. (4.12)

For Wittgenstein, this attempt to stand "outside" the world is equivalent to trying to *say* (*sagen*) what can only be *shown* (*gezeigt*).

Propositions [*Der Satz*] *show* [*zeigt*] the logical form of reality. They display it. (4.121)
What *can* be shown, cannot be said [*gesagt*]. (4.1212)

Pictorial form, then, is shown (mirrored, displayed, reflected), and hence cannot be said (stated, asserted, described, pictured). This distinction between saying and showing is a crucial one in the *Tractatus* and must never be confused. What can be said is not shown, and what is shown cannot be said; the two concepts never merge or overlap. In order to see why Wittgenstein makes this distinction crucial let us ask what it would like to *say* what the logical and pictorial form of propositions is. In the *Notebooks*[10] Wittgenstein asserts that in order to *say* what the logical properties of language are we would need a language which did *not* have these properties. But this is impossible, for such a "language" would be *illogical*. In the Preface to the *Tractatus* Wittgenstein denies the possibility of setting a limit to *thought* (*Denken*) for just these reasons, namely, that "we should have to find both sides of the limit thinkable (i.e. we should have to be able to think what

[10] Ludwig Wittgenstein, *Notebooks 1914-1916*, ed. by G. E. M. Anscombe and G. H. von Wright (Oxford, Basil Blackwell, 1961), Appendix II, p. 107.

cannot be thought)".[11] In other words, in order to say what pictorial form is we would need a language that did not have pictorial form, but such a "language" is impossible because it would be illogical and unthinkable. A language without pictorial form is not a language at all, for the former is the very essence of language and the necessary condition for its possibility.

Conversely, a language *with* pictorial form cannot be the vehicle of saying what logical form is because to do so it would have to refer to *itself.* And this inevitably leads to the semantical and logical paradoxes, which plagued the foundations of logic and mathematics around the turn of the century.[12] The necessary (though perhaps not sufficient) condition for the paradoxes is the possibility that either a concept or proposition can refer to itself, i.e., can *say* something about itself. We can deny this possibility in two ways. One, we can hold that only *another* proposition can assert something about a given proposition, and proceed to construct a hierarchy of such propositions on the model of Russell's theory of types or Carnap's formal and material mode distinction; or second, we can distinguish between the sayable and the unsayable, as Wittgenstein does in his mysticism.

Both alternatives hold that a proposition cannot have self-reference. This view is held to be necessary because of the consequence of the antinomies, and is hence the conclusion of a *reductio ad absurdum.* That is, if we assume that a proposition can be self-referential we get a contradiction; we must therefore deny the premiss that propositions can be self-referential. They differ, however, in that the first view holds that what a proposition cannot say about *itself* can, at least in principle, be said by *another* proposition. Wittgenstein, on the contrary, holds that there are *some* things which are intrinsically *un*sayable — they cannot be said in *any* language. The failure to see this basic difference results

[11] Ludwig Wittgenstein, *Tractatus Logico-Philosophicus,* trans. by Pears and McGuinness (London, Routledge & Kegan Paul, 1961), p. 3.

[12] I do not mean to imply that the paradoxes were necessarily the *motive* for Wittgenstein's mysticism. It is safe to say, however, that mysticism was an *alternative* to a solution which Wittgenstein did not find wholly acceptable, namely, the hierarchy of meta-languages and the infinite regress.

in a general begging of the question in regard to the mysticism in the *Tractatus*. Let me turn to one of the most important of these critics, Carnap, as an example. By examining his attempt to overcome or deny the mystical aspect of Wittgenstein's theory of meaning we will become clearer on what it really means and implies.

This is not the place to go into a detailed and exhaustive account of Carnap's views, but one or two examples of his method of dealing with some of the same philosophical problems that Wittgenstein deals with may be illuminating. All that I intend to do in the following is to *illustrate* how Carnap's approach differs fundamentally from Wittgenstein's, and that what he says is basically incompatible with the *Tractatus*. Thus, I am not concerned with refuting Carnap but with contrasting him with Wittgenstein, and showing that what he proposes as an alternative to the *Tractatus* does not meet the real problems raised there. This should become clearer as I proceed.

In *The Logical Syntax of Language* Carnap summarizes Wittgenstein's mysticism (i.e., the view that the logical form of propositions cannot be expressed (*gesagt*) in any language), and his own position as follows:

> In other words: there are no sentences about the forms of sentences; there is no expressible syntax. In opposition to this view, our construction of syntax has shown that it can be correctly formulated and that syntactical sentences do exist.[13]

These "syntactical sentences" about the logical form of propositions (which together constitute what he calls "logical syntax"),[14] are what Carnap understands to constitute philosophy, once it is freed of the pseudo-questions of traditional metaphysics, epistemology, ethics, etc. [15] The difference between Carnap and Wittgen-

[13] Rudolf Carnap, *The Logical Syntax of Language* (New York, Harcourt, Brace and Co., 1937), p. 282.

[14] Carnap's general definition of logical syntax is as follows. "By the *logical syntax* of a language, we mean the formal theory of the linguistic forms of that language — the systematic statement of the formal rules which govern it together with the development of the consequences which follow from these rules." *Ibid.*, p. 1.

[15] *Ibid.*, p. 277 ff.

stein on this question is crucial. The latter holds that philosophy is an activity, not a theory about either the world *or* language. In particular, for Wittgenstein philosophy aims at the logical clarification (*logische Klärung*) of thoughts (*Gedanke*). Such clarification, however, does not result in a list of "philosophical propositions", and thus philosophy is not a "body of doctrine" (*Lehre*) (4.112). The activity (*Tätigkeit*) of logical analysis clarifies thoughts by setting the limits to what can be thought from *within* the realm of the thinkable. In this way we discover what is *un*thinkable (4.114). From another point of view, this amounts to the same thing as determining the limits of natural science (4.113, 6.52, 6.53). The final result of philosophical activity, then, will be that

> It [philosophy] will signify what cannot be said, by presenting clearly what can be said. (4.115)
>
> Everything that can be thought at all can be thought clearly. Everything that can be put into words can be put clearly. (4.116)

In contrast to Wittgenstein's conception of philosophy as an activity only, Carnap holds that although philosophy (conceived of as the logical syntax of the language of science) does not have any sentences *peculiar* to itself, and which do not form a part of any of the existing natural sciences, it does consist of sentences, albeit purely formal ones.

> ...I agree with Wittgenstein that there are no special sentences of the logic of science (or philosophy). The sentences of the logic of science are formulated as syntactical sentences about the language of science; but no new domain in addition to that of science itself is thereby created.[16]

In short, we may say that Carnap rejects Wittgenstein's mysticism by holding that the logical form of language can be expressed *by* language, and that this is precisely what he calls the legitimate and sole function of philosophy. For Wittgenstein, however, there is not, nor can there be, any such thing as logical syntax. Hence, philosophy is an activity and nothing more; philosophy

[16] *Ibid.*, p. 284.

cannot *say* anything but can merely show (*zeigen*) or elucidate (*erläutern*) (4.12 ff.).

With this rough sketch of Carnap's opposition to Wittgenstein let us see by means of specific examples how he tries to overcome Wittgenstein's mysticism. For Carnap, all theoretical questions are of two kinds, "object-questions" and "logical questions". The former are concerned with the empirical or non-linguistic world, i.e., facts, things, their properties and relations, etc. The latter are concerned with language alone. They are thus purely formal, and deal with problems about the meaning of sentences and terms, their relations and structure, the nature of theories, etc.[17] Corresponding to these two realms — the non-linguistic and the linguistic — there are two modes of speech, the material mode and the formal mode. (Ultimately, of course, all language refers to a non-linguistic realm, since the formal mode refers to the material mode and hence indirectly to that which the latter describes.) In addition to these two modes, however, there is an intermediate class of sentences which *appear* to be object-sentences of the material mode but are actually in the formal mode. These are "pseudo-object-sentences", and it is one of the functions of philosophy to expose their ambiguous status by translating them from the material mode so that they are clearly seen to belong to the formal mode.[18]

Carnap illustrates this technique of translation by taking what he calls "universal words"[19] (in Wittgenstein's terminology, "formal concepts") and translating them into the formal mode whenever they occur in sentences which belong to the material mode. Let us select three important universal words, "thing", "number", and "property",[20] and see how Carnap treats them.

[17] *Ibid.*, p. 277.

[18] *Ibid.*, pp. 284-285.

[19] "We will call a predicate of which every full sentence [in which it occurs] is an analytic sentence a *universal predicate*, or, if it is a word in the word-language, a *universal word*." *Ibid.*, p. 292. Examples of universal words would be the term "color" in the sentence, "Blue is a color", or the term "number", in the sentence, "Seven is a number". (It is clear also that these sentences are analytic.)

[20] These designate are formal concepts for Wittgenstein. (Cite 4.126 and 4.1272).

First, there is the sentence in the material mode:

The moon is a *thing*; five is not a thing, but a number.

Translated into the formal mode it reads:

'Moon' is a thing-word (thing-name); 'five' is not a thing-word, but a number-word.

Similarly, in the case of the universal word "property", the material mode expression is:

A property is not a *thing*.

and its corresponding formal mode translation is:

An adjective (property-word) is not a thing-word.[21]

What has Carnap really done here? First, we see that the expression in the formal mode contains words in inverted commas (i.e., "five", and "moon"), which words do *not* appear in inverted commas in their material mode form. The use of inverted commas is intended to make it explicit that we are talking *about* the *words* as such, not about their "meanings" or designata — that we are *mentioning* the words, not using them. It is thus clear that in the formal mode we are talking about *language*, not facts, things, or properties. (Hence, the difference between saying "Blue is a property" and "'Blue' is a predicate".) But this use of inverted commas has a curious result which may easily be overlooked. This is the second point about Carnap's translation to which I wish to call attention. The use of inverted commas transforms what in the material mode was a *symbol* which is *used* into what in the formal mode is a *sign* which is *mentioned*. When we say "'Five' is a number-word" as opposed to "Five is a number" we are merely referring to the word "five" itself, that is, we are mentioning it *as a word* and not using it to refer to something else. This makes it look as *if* we are talking about the English word "five" and *not* (say) the French word "*cinq*" or the German word "*fünf*". And

[21] Carnap, *op. cit.*, p. 297.

if this is true Carnap's translation applies only to the English language and philosophers who express themselves in that language! But surely Carnap does not intend that what he says in his translation apply to English words only, or indeed to words alone.

This change from using a word to mentioning it is subtle but crucial. As Anscombe points out below, when we ask for (say) a man's name we are not asking for the name of his name. If one were to give the name of his name one would be mentioning it and not using it. But to mention a name is not to use it as a *name*, for the function of names is to refer to non-linguistic entities, not to other names. Let us suppose someone asks me what is the name of a certain man, and that his name is really "Smith". If I reply, "'Smith'" I would not be answering his question, for I would be merely uttering the word. Thus, I would not be *using* the word to *designate* the particular individual in question, i.e., Smith.

> ... I cannot *informatively* be told that this name-of-a name, i.e. "Smith", is the name 'Smith'; if I do not already understand this, I should not understand the statement that it is so.[22]

I cannot be said to *learn* anything new by being told the name of a name of a name... . Yet Carnap certainly intends to give us some information by setting up his linguistic hierarchy based on formal-material mode distinctions.

One of the main purposes of Carnap's material mode-formal mode distinction is to set up the means by which we can talk *about* the formal properties of a language by means of *another* language. In the material mode, words and sentences are *used* to designate non-linguistic reality, and in the formal mode they are *mentioned.* Hence, by mentioning words and sentences in one language it is possible to talk about them in another. In the formal mode the first step is made towards a language about language, or a meta-language. Such a procedure, when completed, would yield what Carnap calls the logical syntax of language. We would thus have a whole hierarchy of languages consisting of what is usually termed

[22] G. E. M. Anscombe, *An Introduction to Wittgenstein's Tractatus* (London, Hutchinson University Library, 1959), pp. 82-84.

the "object language" (the language which functions in a signifying relation to non-linguistic reality), and various meta-languages, each meta-language referring to the language on the previous level and to *no* others, especially not itself. And since there is no inherent restriction on the number of meta-languages possible (the limit usually being set by practical considerations) an infinite hierarchy of meta-languages is possible in principle.

This brings us to the real point of contention between those of Carnap's view and Wittgenstein. In Anscombe's example quoted above the advocates of meta-languages hold that what we do not know, or cannot say, at a given level in the hierarchy can be said and conveyed in some other level. Wittgenstein's mysticism denies this. The fundamental objection to the whole apparatus of metal-languages is that it involves an *infinite regress*; there is no mechanism built into the hierarchy whereby one can stop the regress from one level to another. The reply to this criticism is that the regress, even though it may be infinite or at least unending, is not damaging, for it is always possible in principle to construct a higher level in order to say what cannot be said at a *given* level and the levels previous to it. I will illustrate this by a single example. Let F be a fact in the world; let f be the sentence which describes F; let f_1 be the sentence that describes certain properties of f, and so on to f_n. When we want to say something about F, we assert f; when we want to say something about f we assert f_1, and so on. Now, the critic objects to this procedure by pointing out that it leads to an infinite regress. But the reply by defenders of the language hierarchy is that this does not ultimately matter, for we can talk about *any* chosen level, f_n, by merely constructing $f_n + {}_1$, and also, of course, $f_n —_1$, $f_n —_2$, etc., have all been described. In short, the critic of the regress holds that the fact that the regress is infinite means that *nothing* is explained; whereas its defender says that, although *every* level cannot be described *any given* level can be described, at least in principle. The only limitation to the further construction of levels is a practical one, and hence extrinsic to the mechanism itself. We may call the infinite regress described above a "benign" regress.

On the other hand, Wittgenstein's position asserts that the infinite regress is "vicious". This can be explained as follows. In the hierarchy f, f_1, f_2 ... f_n we cannot understand f_n without *already* understanding f_{n-1}, f_{n-2} ... all the way to f, the first level. The reason for this is that the properties of any given level (f_n) cannot be described in another level (f_{n+1}) because they necessarily appear in *that* level also (i.e., in f_{n+1}). Thus, the understanding of f_{n+1} *presupposes as its necessary condition* an understanding of f_n. But this, *ex hypothesi*, has not been achieved. To recall Anscombe's example, in order to understand the name-of-a-name I must already understand the name itself.

... I cannot *informatively* be told that this name-of-a-name, i.e. "'Smith'", is the name "Smith"; if I do not already understand this, I shall not understand the statement that this is so.[23]

Thus, for Wittgenstein, the infinite regress of meta-languages is "vicious", in that the regress *can never get started* in the first place.

In terms of the *Tractatus*, we cannot form a meta-language to talk about pictorial and logical form because it, *qua* language, would have to have pictorial form. Returning to our hierarchy of meta-languages, f, f_1, f_2 ..., let "*" denote the property of pictorial form which, for Wittgenstein, every language on every level must have. Thus, letting f be any proposition, our hierarchy would look like this:

$$\begin{array}{c} f_n^* \\ . \\ . \\ . \\ f_2^* \\ f_1^* \\ f^* \end{array}$$

(f_n^* is the "highest" level of the hierarchy). Since *every* level has

[23] *Ibid.*, p. 84.

the property * we cannot talk about *any* level, for to do so we would need a level which did *not* have *; but this is impossible, for without * we would have an illogical language, i.e., no language at all. To talk about pictorial form (*) we would have to construct an illogical language, or think the unthinkable.

We are now in a position to understand more exactly what lies at the heart of the opposition between Carnap and Wittgenstein on this point. It will be remembered that the purpose of Carnap's translations into the formal mode is to show explicitly that a sentence or word which *seemed* to be used to talk about non-linguistic reality was actually being used to talk about language. To effect this the word was mentioned (not used) and described by purely linguistic predicates, as in "'Five' is a number-word", or "'Red' is a predicate". Wittgenstein's position, on the other hand, is that universal words (or formal concepts), like number, object, relation, and property, cannot be used *or* mentioned in any sentence without producing nonsense (*unsinnig*). Indeed, for Wittgenstein, the terms "predicate" or "number-word" are just as much formal concepts as their non-linguistic counterparts property and number.[24] *That* a given term is included under a formal concept is *shown* by our symbolism, and cannot be *said* in any language, whether of a meta-level or not.

> When something falls under a formal concept as one of its objects, this cannot be expressed by means of a proposition. Instead it is shown [*es zeigt sich*] in the very sign for this object. (A name shows [*zeigt*] that it signifies an object, a sign for a number that it signifies a number, etc.) (4.126)

A familiar example of this is seen in the traditional conventions for logical symbolism. In order to distinguish clearly between (say) individuals and properties, lower-case letters (a, b, c) are used for the former, and capital letters (M, N, P) for the latter. Similarly, functions are distinguished from variables by the use of Greek capital letters (Ø, Ψ) for the former and lower case italicized Roman letters (*x*, *y*, *z*) for the latter. This avoids confusions between

[24] *Ibid.*, p. 83.

different logical "types" by using a special *kind* of symbol for different formal concepts. There is thus no *need* to *say* that something falls under a given formal concept (as Carnap thought) because this can easily be *seen* from the signs themselves and our symbolic conventions (assuming, of course, they are unambiguous).

Thus, Wittgenstein's notion of showing and the mystical is a *total rejection* of the very possibility of even beginning the regress of meta-languages or of constructing a formal mode of discourse. For Wittgenstein, the *function* which Carnap's formal mode performs is replaced by a proper symbolism which *shows* the formal properties of language. This in effect renders Carnap's technique ultimately superfluous (given an adequate symbolism). But Wittgenstein's objection goes much deeper, since there cannot be another language which *says* what these formal properties are, because it itself would presuppose them. And in addition to the general objections against Carnap's position raised by Wittgenstein's mysticism and his notion of showing there are those resulting from the use of inverted commas. The latter are internal to Carnap's technique, and whereas the former (mysticism) is in a sense external (in that it is a product of another philosophical position) it is enough for the purposes of this chapter to have shown *that* Wittgenstein cannot accept Carnap's alternative and *why* he cannot. The difference between Wittgenstein and Carnap on this point is, I think, one so basic that it requires a great deal of effort for one even to understand the other. If each fails in this attempt, however, the criticisms offered will inevitably be irrelevant and question begging, and genuine philosophical argument and dialogue will break down. Thus, it may not be too much of an exaggeration to say that ultimately Russell, Carnap and others simply *missed the point* of what Wittgenstein was trying to express in his mysticism. (Unfortunately, such "missing the point" is not uncommon in philosophy.)

The problem of the self-referential character of language and thought has a long history in philosophy. Its most conspicuous first appearance is no doubt in Plato's *Parmenides*, in which Plato, through the person of Parmenides, raises a series of purported objections against his own theory of Forms.[25] The objection which is relevant to the present discussion is that which is commonly termed the "third Man" argument. The argument is crucial to the problem of Wittgenstein's mysticism because its force as an *argument* rests on the assumption of the possibility of self-reference in language. That is, assuming that the Forms are self-referential, an infinite regress is necessarily engendered once the Forms are posited. The argument runs basically as follows. (1) Many particular great things have a character in common, Greatness, by virtue of which they possess the property great. (2) Now if we admit that Greatness *itself* can be great, then the many particulars *plus* the Form will have a common character, which common character will in turn lead to the positing of a "third" Form. That is, since Greatness is itself great it becomes another *member* of the class of great things, and the same reasons for asserting the existence of the first Form will lead us to assert that of the second, and so on *ad infinitum.*[26]

The force of this argument rests on the point that the Forms do not explain what they are allegedly intended to explain, for the supposition of their existence leads to an infinite regress. In other words, the claim by Parmenides is that the regress is *vicious.* Since the Forms are self-referential we must in every case posit a "third Man", but this means that the Forms do not explain the *original* relationship between *particulars,* the latter being the whole point of positing the Forms in the first place. This makes it clear

[25] The problems of exegesis arising from this dialogue are, of course, extensive. For instance, there are problems as to how seriously Plato took these criticisms; whether they were his own or those of others; how damaging they are; or even whether Plato felt they were *relevant* to his theory as he himself understood it. I cannot try to answer these questions here since they are far beyond the scope of this book, nor is this necessary for my present purpose.

[26] Plato, *Parmenides*, in *The Dialogues of Plato*, Vol. II, trans. by B. Jowett (New York, Random House, 1937), 132. The notion that a Form has self-reference might be caused at least in part by an ambiguity of "is". E.g., a man is a Man (partakes of Man), but Man is not *a* man. Man does not "have" the character Man as particulars do, but *is* that character: Man is (=) Man. That is, the regress results from treating the Form as a *thing*. Thus, it is asserted that a Form *has* a character in the *same* way a particular has it.

that the regress is presented as a vicious one, and not benign. Otherwise, Socrates would merely *admit* to Parmenides that a "third Man" was necessary, and a "fourth Man", etc. That is, if the regress were felt to be benign Parmenides' argument would not be an *objection* to the theory of Forms, but merely an indication of one of its *implications*.

The third Man argument in the *Parmenides* is similar to the argument raised by monists against the reality of relations. The argument rests on the possibility that a relation (or in the case of Plato, a Form) can itself be a *term* in a relation. We saw earlier in Chapter II (in regard to 3.1432) that Daitz, Evans, and Stenius also asserted this, thereby destroying the isomorphism of picture and fact necessary for the picture theory. We also saw that Wittgenstein denied the assumption that relations can be terms (objects), because relation-signs are not names and hence relations are not objects. Instead, the existence of a relation is *shown* in a proper symbolism. In the same way, we may add now that language cannot refer to itself. Wittgenstein expresses this by saying that a function cannot be its own argument: Ø cannot fill the empty argument place in Ø ( ) (3.333).

In short, Wittgenstein's notion of showing — his mysticism — is a radical philosophical denial of the self-referential character of language, and hence of the infinite regress and hierarchy of types and meta-languages. And as such it provides the key for the solution of the Platonic problem of "participation". This solution is analogous to that proposed by Aristotle. That is, the notion of showing achieves the same end that Aristotle sought to accomplish by putting the forms "in" the things.[27] Asserting that the facts *show* their logical form is just another way of asserting that it is *in* them (the facts), or of denying the necessity of talking about a realm of "meanings" distinct and apart from the world.

[27] This path is pursued further in the *Philosophical Investigations*, where Wittgenstein comes even closer to an Aristotalian conception of meaning and thought. In the later work the notions of language games and "looking for the use" become essential, in place of objects and pictures.

The above parallel with Plato was not intended to be of mere historical interest. Rather, it will serve, I hope, as the basis for my general conclusions on Wittgenstein's mysticism and theory of meaning. The first of these conclusions is that there is a distinctly Platonic element in Wittgenstein's conception of language and meaning. This Platonism may be expressed by saying that for Wittgenstein meaning is not a *fact* in the world.

This may seem to contradict the assertion made earlier that pictures are facts. But it will be remembered that it is only as a *sign*, not as a *symbol*, that a picture can be called a fact. Further, what is characteristic and essential to a picture *qua* picture is its pictorial form, and this is a property of the picture as symbol, i.e., of the picture as a proposition.

So a picture, conceived in this way, also includes the pictorial relationship, which makes it into a picture. (2.1413)

We also noted earlier that some facts can *become* picture-facts.[28] But we cannot *say* (*sagen*) that this is so. That is, "P is a picture" is not a significant proposition, for it treats P as a *fact*, hence implying that it can refer to itself, i.e., say about itself that it has the property of being-a-picture. P as a *proposition* cannot be a term in another proposition.[29] To deny this would be to treat the picture as a fact, i.e., something signified by another proposition. But this is incompatible with Wittgenstein's whole position, and hence we can never *say* that a given fact is or is not a picture. This must be *shown* in its application and use.[30]

[28] This implies an element of Aristotelianism. Another Aristotelian element in the *Tractatus* is that structure (*Struktur*) is actual and concrete — it is "in" the world — whereas pictorial form, which is the possibility of structure, is abstract. (Cite Maslow, *op. cit.*, p. 85.)

[29] This is parallel to Wittgenstein's denial in 5.541 (the analysis of "A says p") that a proposition *qua* symbol can be the real predicate of a sentence, that one can have a mental *relation* towards a proposition, as Russell and Moore thought. (Of course, *if* we could have a mental relation towards a proposition-symbol then it would be a *term* in the proposition asserting this relation.)

[30] G. D. O'Brien, *Meaning and Fact: A Study in the Philosophy of Wittgenstein*, unpublished doctoral dissertation, University of Chicago, 1960, pp. 90-1.

The *application* of logic decides what elementary propositions there are. What belongs to its application, logic cannot anticipate. (5.557)

Meanings do not lie in the world waiting to be discovered by perceptual observation, as the positivists thought. They are not actual or concrete "things".

... Meanings lie outside the world. If this were not the case then the *meaning* of a proposition would depend on what happened. In order to know whether a proposition had meaning we would have to know the truth of some other proposition.[31]

It is especially important to realize that for Wittgenstein meaning cannot be anything *mental*. One of the primary purposes of the *Tractatus* is to divorce psychology *completely* from logic, theory of meaning, and philosophy. Interpreters and critics who think of the pictures (*Bilder*) of Wittgenstein's picture theory as images or "ideas" in one's mind are psychologizing, and hence grossly distorting Wittgenstein's real views. Nor are meanings "things". Logic, and hence pictorial form, are not to be thought of as entities existing independent and "alongside" of the world of facts.

And if this were not so, how could we apply logic? We might put it this way: if there would be a logic even if there were no world, how then could there be a logic given that there is a world? (5.5521)

If logic were thought as of independent of the *existence* of the world it would be a kind of "fact" that the world had to agree or disagree with, or a "thing" that the world had to "partake" of (as in Plato).[32] But logic "sets the limits to the world" — it *itself* is the test of the agreement and disagreement of facts. If it did not do this it would not be logic.[33]

This provides the key to the so-called problem of the relationship between thought and reality. Meaning relates to possibilities

[31] *Ibid.*, pp. 64-65. (Cf. also *Tractatus*, 4.064, 2.0211).

[32] We could ask, for instance, "Is the world logical?" thinking that we could imagine what the world would be *like* if it were not. That is, we would believe we could imagine two worlds, side by side, a logical and an illogical one, and then try to decide which the real world we live in is. But for Wittgenstein this is absurd.

[33] Anscombe, *op. cit.*, p. 165.

as these are expressed by pictorial and logical form. The latter are also defined as the "form of reality" (2.18), a sign being able to picture any reality with which it shares its logical form (2.171).[34] The logical form is hence what is *common* to thought and reality. The expression of possibilities inherent in logical form also shows that it is not an *actuality* existing "alongside" and independent of the actuality of facts. It is this paradigm of two independently existing actualities, conceived of as wholly different in nature, that engenders the *duality* of thought and reality, and hence the problem of relating them, or of showing how the one can "partake" of the other (Plato). Thus, the concept of pictorial form enables Wittgenstein to overcome, or rather *dissolve*, this duality, for by means of pictorial form

Signs in their operation refer to the actual world only *via* the reference to the framework of possibilities of which the historical world is the actualization.[35]

I will now conclude my discussion of Wittgenstein's mysticism, In this chapter I have tried to emphasize the crucial importance of the mystical in Wittgenstein's theory of meaning. I have done this by explaining how it develops out of the nature of logical and pictorial form. By means of the distinction between saying and showing it was seen that nothing could be said about the logical form of language because this saying would have to be done by means of language, and any language, *qua* language, possesses logical form. We cannot "transcend" language in order to talk about its logical properties. Thus, it was necessary to reject such attempts at "transcendence" as those of Carnap, since the formal mode of description presupposes the very characteristics which it is intended to describe. Wittgenstein's mysticism can therefore be seen as a radical and total rejection of the possibility of a hierarchy of meta-languages. I tried to explicate this rejection in terms of the notion of a vicious (as opposed to benign) infinite

[34] *Ibid.*, p. 75.
[35] O'Brien, *op. cit.*, p. 65.

regress. For Wittgenstein, *any* regress or hierarchy of languages is necessarily vicious, and not benign as the proponents of the hierarchy claim. This viciousness of the regress is simply another way of saying that pictorial form can only be *shown,* since any attempt to say (i.e., describe) what it is necessarily presupposes it. Hence, language cannot be self-referential. The logical properties of language cannot refer to themselves nor be described by another language. Indeed, this is not necessary, for a correct symbolism would reveal (show) what these properties are. Finally, the key for the solution of the problem of the relationship between thought and reality was provided by the denial that meaning is a fact or actuality. Since meaning is not actual there are not two actualities (thought and the world) which have to be "brought together".

I will now turn to the second major section of this book, which deals with truth. First, however, it is necessary to take up the problems of negation and negative facts.

V

NEGATION AND NEGATIVE FACTS

> Here is a deep mystery.
> It is the mystery of negation: This is not how things are, and yet we can say *how* things are *not*.[1]

In this chapter and the one following I will discuss Wittgenstein's theory of truth and falsity. But before taking up the positive nature of this theory (which will be done in Chapter VI) it is necessary to develop in detail two crucial problems, those of negation and negative facts. These will be treated, however, only to the extent that they are directly relevant to the theory of truth. In particular, I am concerned in the present chapter to demonstrate one main assertion, namely, that what Wittgenstein means by a negative fact (*negativ Tatsache*) and his contention that every elementary proposition has only one negation are ultimately merely two aspects of the same problem. This will raise two subsidiary problems: (1) that of showing that every elementary proposition *must* have one and only one negation; and (2) the definition of the *nature* of negative facts. The main points to be discussed in connection with the above are the following.

First, I will call attention to the distinction between negative statements and false statements, since this distinction can easily be overlooked. I will then try to show *why* Wittgenstein must hold that elementary propositions have one and only one negation. To do so, I will show the difficulties which result from the denial of this view. Next, the two notions of contradiction and exclusion will be treated, mainly within the context of the problem of the logical independence of *Sachverhalte*. I will take the position that

[1] Ludwig Wittgenstein, *Notebooks 1914-1916*, ed. by G. E. M. Anscombe and G. H. von Wright (Oxford, Basil Blackwell, 1961), p. 30e.

some of Wittgenstein's own views on this question are not wholly satisfactory and will suggest an alternative which appears to be consistent with the general doctrines of the *Tractatus*. This alternative consists basically of asserting that two elementary propositions can exclude (though not contradict) one another, and of substituting the familiar notion of contrariety as the meaning of exclusion. This will in turn necessitate a discussion of Wittgenstein's notions of logical space and logical place. At this point it should become clear that the doctrine of negative facts is indispensable for the solution of the problem of defining the single negation of elementary propositions.

In beginning my discussion of negative facts I will discuss an alternative theory suggested by Demos. I will try to show that Demos' attempt to deny the necessity of negative facts by substituting the notion of the *opposition* of *positive* propositions does not meet the problem Wittgenstein is concerned with, namely, the necessity of holding that an elementary proposition has only *one* negation. After pointing out what I feel to be the chief merits of Demos' view (in contrast to Russell's) I will conclude by giving Wittgenstein's own definition of a negative fact. By this time I hope it will be clear that the latter ultimately constitutes the meaning of negation as applied to elementary propositions. That is, I hope to have shown that a negative fact is to be defined as *the* negation of an elementary proposition. I shall now begin with the question of negation.

NEGATION

I propose to base my discussion on the following two statements:

... Every proposition [*Satz*] has one and only one negative, since there is only one proposition that lies completely outside it. (5.513)

The existence and non-existence of states of affairs [*Sachverhalte*] is reality [*Wirklichkeit*].

(We also call the existence of states of affairs a positive fact [*Tatsache*], and their non-existence a negative fact [*Tatsache*]. (2.06)

First, to avoid possible confusion, I would like to make a clarification. The reader must keep in mind that the problem of negation and negative facts is distinct from that of falsehood, although in some respects they are closely related and frequently overlap. The failure to see this distinction clearly gives rise to the temptation to define falsehood as "saying that which is (=exists) not". And the next step is that since "saying that which is not" is impossible (for we are talking about "nothing") false statements are also impossible. Thus, all *meaningful* statements are necessarily true, and all "false" statements are meaningless, hence not really false at all. But such consequences are obviously unsatisfactory and explain nothing. We must, then, from the outset, make a clear distinction between negative and false statements.

The distinction between them can be easily seen when we keep in mind the obvious fact that a negative statement can be either true *or* false; a negative statement is not by definition a false one. This, at least, is the assumption of common sense and ordinary language. It could be denied (as it was by the Sophists), but for now I merely ask the reader to assume its possibility for the purpose of following my exposition without confusion. I hope that my subsequent remarks will (1) show that the distinction *is* possible, and (2) supply an adequate account of its nature.

The proper antithesis of negative statements is positive statements, as that of false statements is true statements. Thus, there is no strict parallel between negative and false on the one hand, and positive and true on the other. Also, it would be convenient for purposes of exegesis to separate the discussion of negation and negative statements from that of negative facts, but I do not think this can be satisfactorily done. My main reason for thinking this is that one of the essential characteristics of the doctrine of negation in the *Tractatus* is that every elementary proposition has one and only one negative, and that this expresses what Wittgenstein means by a negative fact. Thus, I propose to discuss 5.513 and 2.06 (quoted above) together, hoping that their intimate connection will become apparent as I proceed. Finally, I distinguish between the problem of negation and that of negative statements because the mere presence of the negation *sign* is *not* necessarily definitive of a negative statement, and hence a statement in which it occurs does not necessarily describe a negative fact.[2]

I stated earlier that my specific thesis in this chapter is that statements 5.513 and 2.06 really express two aspects of the same doctrine. That is, I wish to assert that a negative fact and the notion that every elementary proposition has one and only one negation are basically two aspects of the *same* doctrine, i.e., a *negativ Tatsache is* the single negation of an *Elementarsatz*. But first, let me further clarify the problem before I continue. The *Satz* which Wittgenstein says has one and only one negation is and must be an *Elementarsatz*.

In order to see *why* every elementary proposition must have one and only one negation let us assume that this is *not* the case, i.e., let us assume that an elementary proposition can have two or more (perhaps an infinity) of negations. If this were so, then to assert a given elementary proposition p as true would *exclude* all its negations, i.e., imply their falsehood. Let -p and q be two such negations of p. Then given that p is true q is necessarily false. Thus, the falsehood of q is *inferred* from the truth of p. This, however, conflicts with Wittgenstein's doctrine that two elementary propositions cannot contradict one another (6.3751). Correspondingly, the independence of *Sachverhalte* would be undermined.

States of affairs are independent of one another. (2.061)
From the existence or non-existence of one state of affairs it is impossible to infer the existence or non-existence of another. (2.062)

This is the basic principle of Wittgenstein's pluralism. If we were to hold that the falshood of q could be inferred from the truth of p this would mean that we could infer the non-existence of one state of affairs — that described by q — from the existence of another — that described by p. I think these considerations are

[2] G. E. M. Anscombe, *An Introduction to Wittgenstein's Tractatus* (London, Hutchinson University Library, 1959), p. 34.

sufficient to indicate *why* the doctrine of 5.513 that every elementary proposition has one and only one negation is needed. But it is at this point that problems begin to arise.

In his brief article "Some Remarks on Logical Form", written about ten years after the publication of the *Tractatus*, Wittgenstein asserts:

> I maintain that the statement which attributes a degree to a quality cannot further be analyzed. ...
> The mutual exclusion of unanalyzable statements of degree contradicts an opinion which was published by me several years ago and which necessitated that atomic propositions could not exclude one another. I here deliberately say 'exclude' and not 'contradict', for there is a difference between these two notions, and atomic propositions, although they cannot contradict, may exclude one another.[3]

Wittgenstein goes on to say that he *used* to think that a proposition asserting a difference of degree to a color could be further analyzed into two propositions joined by conjunction, "as I could describe the contents of my pocket by saying 'It contains a penny, a shilling, two keys, and nothing else'".[4] For instance, let E be a color, and b its degree; then to say that E has two degrees of color would be expressed thus: E(b) & E(b). But since this means simply E(b) the analysis will not express what he intended it to. (Wittgenstein gives two other alternative analyses which he also rejects.) Hence, he concludes that such statements are really *un*analyzable and therefore elementary.[5] But the problem arises that *if* two color

[3] Wittgenstein, *op. cit.*, p. 168. Wittgenstein is obviously referring to section 6.3751 of the *Tractatus*. There, the German term which is translated as "contradiction" is "*Kontradiction*". In context it is opposed to "*Tautologie*" or "tautology"; it is thus clear that Wittgenstein is referring to what is normally meant by "logical contradiction". In another place, 4.211, where Wittgenstein says that two elementary propositions cannot contradict one another, the German phrase is "*in Widerspruch stehen*", which also normally means "to contradict". I can find no place in the *Tractatus* where Wittgenstein uses a word meaning "exclude" as *distinct* from "to contradict" or "contradiction". Thus, if Wittgenstein *did* distinguish between the two at the time of the *Tractatus* there is no direct evidence for this in the text.

[4] *Ibid.*, p. 167.

[5] *Ibid.*, pp. 167-168.

statements of this kind are elementary, and since the assertion that a given color has two degrees of intensity at the same time, or is in two places at the same time, is "contradictory", it would follow that two elementary propositions can contradict one another and hence are *not independent*. Needless to say, this is a serious difficulty. Now, Wittgenstein admits that the above color statements are impossible to conjoin, but he says that they do not strictly *contradict* one another, but rather *exclude* one another. He explains this "exclusion" as follows.

To say that two propositions exclude one another means that, in the case of the logical product of these two propositions, we cannot have the instance where *both* are true and their product false. That is, there can be no *first* line in the matrix for exclusion. This differs from contradiction in that in the latter *all* the lines *appear* in the matrix but all are false. Thus, for two propositions, p and q, we write:

Exclusion

p	q	
T	F	F
F	T	F
F	F	F

Contradiction

p	q		
T	T	F	← (This line does *not* appear in the exclusion matrix.)
T	F	F	
F	T	F	
F	F	F	

The above analysis[6] strikes one immediately as suspicious. And further investigation I think makes it clear that it will not do. That is, I do not believe that this *way* of expressing the distinction between exclusion and contradiction can be valid. I base this contention on Wittgenstein's own views. Wittgenstein says that the reason why the first line in the exclusion matrix cannot appear is because there can be no *fact* in the world which expresses this possibility, and not simply because we cannot write it there. But if this is to guide the construction of our matrices and hence the

[6] *Ibid.*, pp. 168-171.

range of truth-possibilities, then for the same reason we cannot write *any* line in the contradiction matrix, for no line can express a fact because each is a contradiction.

In many ways it is hard to understand what Wittgenstein is trying to do in "Some Remarks on Logical Form", and especially to see it in its proper relation to the *Tractatus*. Basically, what Wittgenstein *wants* to do is to maintain the independence of elementary propositions against the difficulties raised by contradictory color statements. For *if* the latter are elementary it would be possible that one elementary proposition be *inferred* from another, since in a contradiction, if p and q contradict one another we know that one is false if the other is true, and vice versa. Correspondingly, the independence of states of affairs would also be threatened. In Chapter II I argued that the two color statements "This is red" and "This is brown" could *not* be elementary propositions (since properties are not objects, and the predicates "red" and "brown" are claimed to denote properties). Wittgenstein himself says that color statements cannot be elementary.

It is clear that the logical product of two elementary propositions can neither be a tautology nor a contradiction. The statement that a point in the visual field has two different colors at the same time is a contradiction. (6.3751)

Hence, in the *Tractatus* Wittgenstein thought that color statements were *not* elementary, but later thought that they *were*, and this change of mind necessitated a distinction between exclusion and contradiction. Thus, in both the *Tractatus* and "Some Remarks" Wittgenstein says elementary propositions cannot contradict one another, though in the latter he says they can exclude one another.

Having made color statements elementary in the later essay Wittgenstein comes closer to logical positivism and logical atomism. This represents a major shift in point of view, for at the time of the *Tractatus* Wittgenstein felt it was not part of his function as a philosopher to give *examples* of elementary propositions or states of affairs. This was a matter for epistemology or psychology, which have nothing to do with philosophy (4.1121). Thus, on his own principles he would not have to say that a *given* proposition is or is not an instance of an elementary proposition. Indeed, one wonders why Wittgenstein did not simply assert, as he did in the *Tractatus*, that color statements were not elementary. This would make much of the argument and apparatus of "Some Remarks" unnecessary. That he did not take this way out can only be explained by his rejecting some of the views of the *Tractatus* and by leaning towards positivism. However, these conjectures on Wittgenstein's philosophical "evolution" are a digression, and I will accordingly return to the problem of the independence of elementary propositions, and in particular the notion of exclusion. Although I rejected Wittgenstein's explanation of exclusion in "Some Remarks" I would like to assert that it seems to me clear that elementary propositions must and indeed do *exclude* (though not contradict) one another. In addition, I wish to give an alternative account of exclusion to that in "Some Remarks", which I think is wholly consistent with the general doctrines of the *Tractatus*.

We saw above that the assumption that an elementary proposition has more than one negation leads to the possibility that of two different elementary propositions, p and q, the falsehood of one (q) could be inferred from the truth of the other (p). This, however, conflicts with Wittgenstein's view that elementary propositions are logically independent of one another, as are the states of affairs they represent. These conclusions enabled us to see the necessity of asserting that an elementary proposition has one and only one negation, i.e., -p only.

In the following discussion I would like to suggest that the familiar notion of logical *contrariety* be given as the meaning of exclusion, so that when we say that two elementary propositions exclude one another (as opposed to contradict) what we mean is that they are contraries. (Two propositions are defined as contraries when they cannot both be true, whereas two propositions are contradictories if, when the one is true the other must be false, and vice versa.) A proposition has only *one* contradictory, but can have any number of contraries. That is, there is only one proposition which, if false, proves that the other is true, but there can be more than one proposition which, if true, shows that the other proposition (or propositions) cannot *also* be true. In order to clarify the notion of exclusion and to explain how states of affairs exclude one another it is necessary to discuss Wittgenstein's notion of logical space (*logische Raum*) and logical place (*logische Ort*).

A proposition determines a place in logical space. The existence of this logical place is guaranteed by the mere existence of the constituents —by the existence of the proposition with sense. (3.4)

The propositional sign with logical co-ordinates — that is the logical place. (3.41)

In geometry and logic alike, a place is a possibility: something can exist in it. (3.411)

A proposition can determine only one place in logical space: nevertheless the whole of logical space must already be given by it. (3.42)

In the above Wittgenstein draws a striking (and, I think, extremely fruitful) analogy between logical space and physical space. The purpose of the analogy is to explain the logical properties and relationships of elementary propositions to one another, just as the earlier analogy with space (2.013) was intended to explain the logical relationship between objects and facts (See Chapter I).

For Wittgenstein, the world (*die Welt*) consists of different "dimensions" or realms of possibility. The states of affairs of one dimension are always totally independent of those of another, although *within* a given dimension the existence of certain facts "excludes" that of others. Each dimension is determined by logical space, or rather helps to make up logical space, and comprises a system of states of affairs which excludes the system of states of affairs of another dimension. According to Stenius, whose analysis I will draw upon in the present discussion:

A combination of atomic states of affairs which consists of one atomic state of affairs of each dimension determines a "possible world", i.e., a possible state of affairs of the world as a whole.[7]

[7] Erik Stenius, *Wittgenstein's Tractatus: A Critical Exposition of its Main Lines of Thought* (Oxford, Basil Blackwell, 1960), p. 43.

In other words,

... A world has as many dimensions as it has mutually independent components of description.[8]

A complete description of the world would be given (at least in part) by indicating which states of affairs (*Sachverhalte*) are facts (*Tatsachen*) in each dimension.[9] Since a *Sachverhalt* is a possible fact (*Tatsache*), a realm of possibility — a dimension of logical space — is a *class* of *Sachverhalte*.

The world can be one in which all states of affairs are independent if and only if each dimension has only *two* values. If this is the case, the assertion of one value would be equivalent to the denial of the other. There could be thus only one existent state of affairs in *each* dimension. On the other hand, in a world in which each dimension has *more* than two values, the assertion of one state of affairs would merely *exclude* the others, thus leaving open the possibility of the existence of more than one state of affairs in a given dimension.[10] For example, in a world of three values, denoted respectively by 1, 0, and $^1/_2$, the denial of (say) 1 would not necessarily tell us whether 0 or $^1/_2$ or both could be asserted.

The sum total of states of affairs determines logical space, logical space being the space of possible states of affairs, or of "possible worlds".

Now the different atomic states of affairs in (p) [p = *all* states of affairs] determine the dimensions of the logical space, and this means that, though only one division holds for the real word, there are neverheless other divisions which are *logically* possible. And each logically possible division defines a *possible world* in the logical space of (p).[11]

In the same way, "... the individual 'places' of the logical space are places of possible worlds (or facts)." For a world of three

[8] *Ibid.*, p. 40.
[9] *Ibid.*, p. 43.
[10] *Ibid.*, p. 44 ff.
[11] *Ibid.*, p. 52.

states of affairs there would be 2^3, or 8 logical places.[12] The "2" in the formula represents the two values of each state of affairs, i.e., its dimension — existent or non-existent (depending on whether the elementary propositions which describe them are true or false) — and the "3" stands for the number of states of affairs comprising *all* the dimensions of logical space.

The situation is exactly parallel to the designation of the truth-values of a class of propositions in a truth-table, for the truth-table merely sets forth or "shows" (*zeigt*) the possible truth-values a given proposition or class of propositions can have. Thus, each combination of truth-values "pictures" a possible world. For example, let us consider our world of three dimensions (each dimension having two values) consisting of the three states of affairs P, Q, and R, denoted respectively by the elementary propositions p, q, and r.

p	q	r
T	T	T
T	T	F
T	F	T
T	F	F
F	T	T
F	T	F
F	F	T
F	F	F

Each horizontal row represents a possible truth-value combination, and hence a possible place in logical space — a possible world — for the corresponding states of affairs.

If p, q, and r are related by logical constants into a compound proposition, e.g., (p & q) ⊃ r, we get the following result:

(p	&	q)	⊃	r
T	T	T	T	T
T	T	T	F	F
T	F	F	T	T
T	F	F	T	F

Here, for the eight places of logical space there is *one* place in which (p & q) ⊃ r is false (i.e., the fact that (p & q) ⊃ r does not exist), and seven places where (p & q) ⊃ r is true (i.e., the fact that (p & q) ⊃ r exists).

[12] *Ibid.*, p. 55.

F	F	T	T	T
F	F	T	T	F
F	F	F	T	T
F	F	F	F	F

The analogue of logical and physical space is now clear. In regard to 3.411, Stenius says:

> ... Just as the 'geometrical position' is a position that a body might occupy and in this sense means a possibility for the existence of a body, the logical position means a 'possibility for the existence of worlds'.[13]

And just as we cannot "jump" from one place in space to another without passing through an intermediate place so we cannot *deduce* a state of affairs of one dimension from that of another, for each dimension is logically independent of the other.

Having clarified the concepts of logical place and space we are in a position to understand what Wittgenstein means when he asserts:

> A proposition can determine only one place in logical space: nevertheless the whole of logical space must already be given by it.
>
> (The force of the proposition reaches through the whole of logical space.) (3.42)

A place in space in the condition for the existence of a physical body, and a place in logical space is the condition for the possibility of a state of affairs. In the *Notebooks* Wittgenstein draws the following diagram,

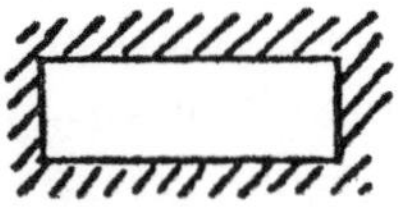

about which he says:

> The proposition, the picture, the model are — in the negative sense — like a solid body restricting the freedom of movement of others, in the positive sense, like the space bounded by solid substance, in which there is room for a body.[14]

[13] *Ibid.*, p. 55.

[14] Wittgenstein, *op. cit.*, p. 30e. (Cf. *Tractatus*, 4.463).

The open space in the second diagram is a logical place which can be "filled" by a positive elementary proposition, the shaded area in the first diagram being the logical place filled by a negative proposition. Further, the shaded area in the second diagram surrounding the open space is the rest of logical space, all of which is *excluded* by that positive elementary proposition. Thus, the open space is p and the shaded area surrounding it is -p, -p being the *whole* of logical space lying *outside* p, i.e., every proposition *excluded* by p.

> One could say that negation must be related to the logical place determined by the negated proposition.
>
> The negating proposition determines a logical place with the help of the logical place of the negated proposition. For it describes it as lying outside the latter's logical place. (4.0641)

> Or rather 'p' and '-p' are like a picture and the infinite plane outside this picture. (Logical place).
>
> I can construct the infinite space outside only by using the picture to bound that space.[15]

There is a logical parallel to what we have said concerning *propositions* in the theory of *classes*. Just as a proposition and its denial (p & -p) determine the whole of logical space, so a given class (say) A and its complement $\bar{A}$ determine the universe class. And just as -p does not designate by *name* those positive propositions excluded by (or even merely other than) p, so $\bar{A}$ does not *name* all those classes which lie outside A, but which together with it make up the whole universe of discourse. For example, in a universe of discourse containing only living creatures, A is the class of men and $\bar{A}$ the class of non-men. But the class of non-men is not a class of the same *type* as that of men. Rather, it is the class of all those other classes (e.g., horses, birds, lions, etc.) which lie outside the class of men. $\bar{A}$ is not identical with the latter, nor can it be reduced to them. (Cf. my later discussion of Demos in the next section of this chapter.)

Our problem may now be specified as follows. From the

[15] *Ibid.*, p. 28e.

above it *seems* that -p is really *identical* with all the propositions which we formally said merely *excluded* p, i.e., the logical sum of *all* the contraries of p seem equal to -p. Hence, although we have succeeded in clarifying the notion of exclusion we seem to have done so at the risk of breaking down the distinction between the negation of a proposition as that which *contradicts* it and those propositions which are merely *contraries* of that proposition. I said earlier that a proposition can only have *one* negation that contradicts it, however many contrary propositions may be excluded from it. Thus, it is necessary at this point to reassert the view that an elementary proposition has one and only one negation, and in doing so to distinguish between -p and all other propositions, that, like -p, are excluded from p, but do not strictly contradict it, and hence cannot be properly called its negation. This requires that I turn to the difficult and paradoxical question of negative facts (*negative Tatsachen*).

NEGATIVE FACTS

Wittgenstein talks about negative facts in two main places in the *Tractatus*. In the first he says:

> The existence and non-existence of states of affairs [*Sachverhalte*] is reality.
>
> (We also call the existence of states of affairs a positive fact, and their non-existence a negative fact.) (2.06)

The second place he mentions negative facts is in connection with an analogy.[16]

> An analogy to illustrate the concept of truth: imagine a black spot on white paper; you can describe the shape of the spot by saying, for each point on the sheet, whether it is black or white. To the fact that a point is black there corresponds a positive fact, and to the fact that a point is white (not black), a negative fact. (4.063)

[16] Compare this analogy to the diagram from the *Notebooks* quoted above. The open and shaded areas of the latter correspond (respectively) to the black dot and white paper of the former.

In this chapter I have been arguing for the thesis that what Wittgenstein means by a negative fact is identical with the view that every elementary proposition has one and only one negation; that a negative fact *is* this unique negation. And we have seen that if this were not so the logical independence of elementary propositions and states of affairs would be impossible. Many philosophers strongly object to the notion of a negative fact on the grounds that it is intuitively absurd or self-contradictory, and is not necessary for an adequate explanation of the notions of truth and falsehood. This view is well worked out and argued for by Demos.[17]

I would like to summarize Demos' position in order to (1) show that his doctrine is inadequate in at least one crucial respect, and (2) relate it to Wittgenstein's own position and show how he overcomes these inadequacies.

First of all, Demos points out that the character of a proposition which makes it positive or negative is not dependent on any relation the proposition might have to the person uttering or writing it. One does not negate or affirm a proposition by adopting a certain mental "attitude" towards it.[18] This, of course, is quite correct. Demos goes on to say that the main reason why there are no negative facts is simply that we never meet with one in *experience* — all our experience is of positive facts, and hence all our knowledge of negative facts is derived from them. This serves as a warning that a negative proposition cannot be "taken at its face value", for it *appears* to assert a fact in the *same way* a positive proposition does, but this cannot be so because there are only positive facts. (Here, the two pairs — positive propositions and positive facts, and negative propositions and negative facts — are exactly parallel.)

Granting that there are no negative facts, then, in so far as a negative

[17] Raphael Demos, "A Discussion of a Certain Type of Negative Proposition", *Mind*, XXVI, No. 101 (January 1917), pp. 188-196.
[18] *Ibid.*, p. 188.

proposition is asserted of a fact at all, the term of reference must be the world of positive facts.[19]

Having distinguished between positive and negative facts Demos goes on to give an account of negative facts and propositions in order to show *why* it is not necessary to assert the existence of negative facts.

He holds that when we negate a proposition we negate it as a *whole*, and not just a part of it. For instance, if I want to negate "All Russians are communists", I should write "Not: All Russians are communists", instead of "All Russians are not communists."[20] The correct formula for negation, then, is: -(---).[21] This shows clearly that the *content* of a negative proposition apart from the "-" sign is positive. Demos is now in a position to define the "process" of negation. He says that the change that takes place in a positive proposition p when it is negated is that there is a "relational modification" of p, and the resulting proposition, -p, means "opposite of" or "contrary to" p.[22] "Opposition" is an "epistemologically primitive" notion, which he defines in the same way as I defined "contrariety" above, namely, as stating that two propositions that are opposed to one another cannot *both* be true.[23]

As the final step in his argument Demos draws an analogy between negative propositions and *descriptions* (as the latter are analyzed by Russell). Just as a description mentions an object without naming it (hence the object is not a constituent of the proposition) so the negative proposition mentions a positive fact

[19] *Ibid.*, p. 189.

[20] This is the distinction between "external" and "internal" negation. As we have seen in Chapter II the distinction is important in the case of description-sentences. As Demos points out, writing "not" before the predicate makes it look as if we were denying the predicate only. But this is misleading because not all propositions are of the subject-predicate form, and because it does not indicate when we are denying the whole proposition or only the ascription of the predicate to the subject. (I should add that the ambiguity in negation arising from the position of the negation-sign in the sentence is present only in the case of *unquantified* sentences.)

[21] Demos, *op. cit.*, pp. 189-190.

[22] *Ibid.*, p. 190.

[23] *Ibid.*, p. 191.

without explicitly referring to it by name. And since there are *several* propositions which are incompatible with a given negative proposition we can regard the latter as an *ambiguous* description, that is, as a proposition containing a phrase of the form: *a* so-and-so.[24] The definition of a negative proposition is thus:

As such, a negative proposition constitutes a description of some true positive proposition in terms of the relation of opposition which the latter sustains to some other positive proposition.

And,

Negative *knowledge* may be defined as knowledge of a true positive proposition by description in terms of its opposition to some other proposition.[25]

Thus, like descriptions, negative propositions are "incomplete symbols" and are hence meaningless unless further defined. They also do not *name* an object, i.e., a negative fact, just as descriptions are not names.[26]

I think that this is a fair and adequate account of Demos' theory, a theory which is in many ways very attractive, especially to philosophers who are partial to Ockham's Razor and to eliminating "undesirable entities" like negative facts. However, I do not believe it is satisfactory, both because of its own intrinsic defects and also because it fails to solve the problem confronting Wittgenstein, namely, that every elementary proposition must have *one and only one* negation.[27] For in effect Demos' denial of negative facts, and in particular his parallel between negative propositions and descriptions, amounts to a denial that a proposition *can* have one and only one negation. Recall that Demos'

[24] *Ibid.*, pp. 191-192.
[25] *Ibid.*, pp. 194-195.
[26] *Ibid.*, p. 195.
[27] Demos, of course, when giving his analysis of negative propositions, was not concerned with a radically pluralistic ontological doctrine to which his analysis had to conform. Thus, it is easy to see how he could have missed the problem bothering Wittgenstein.

definition of "opposition", to which he reduced negative facts, was identical with the definition of contrariety, and hence does not show how one proposition can *contradict* another. In addition, as Russell points out, the notion of incompatibility or opposition poses problems "not so very much simpler than allowing negative facts".[28] A more serious difficulty is, I believe, brought out by a consideration of double negation.

Demos holds that a negative fact (say -P) which "denies" a positive fact (say P) is really merely *another* fact (say Q) which is "incompatible" with P. Hence, proposition -p which describes fact -P is equivalent to q, which describes Q. But if -p ≡ q, then (p & q) ≡ (p & -p). But this cannot be correct, for if we negate -p in (p & -p) we get (p & --p), which is merely (p & p), or p; whereas if we negate q in (p & q) we get (p & -q). Here we see that -p and q are two totally different propositions. When we negate the negative of a proposition we get merely the proposition *itself*, whereas in Demos' example this does not occur, for the second proposition (i.e., q) becomes negative, and not merely equivalent to the first.

Demos' article was written as a reply to Russell's lectures at Harvard in 1914 on logical atomism,[29] in which Russell asserted the existence of negative facts. Thus, Demos' theory can only be properly understood as a criticism of the views put forward by Russell in those lectures. When Russell asserted the existence of negative facts he did so, I believe, in a mistaken and misleading way, and it was this that Demos was really opposed to. Russell said, for instance:

> I have assumed in all that I have said hitherto that there are negative facts, that for example if you say 'Socrates is alive', there is corresponding to that proposition in the real world the fact that Socrates is not alive.[30]

[28] Bertrand Russell, *Logic and Knowledge* (London, George Allen & Unwin Ltd., 1956), p. 213.

[29] These lectures were later reprinted under the title, "The Philosophy of Logical Atomism", in *Logic and Knowledge*, *op. cit.*, pp. 175-283.

[30] Russell, *op. cit.*, p. 211.

And again:

I think you will find that it is simpler to take negative facts as facts, to assume that 'Socrates is not alive' is really an objective fact in the same sense in which 'Socrates is human' is a fact.[31]

From the above it is clear that Russell thinks of negative facts in the same way as positive facts; in Demos' terms, as something that can be met with in "experience", as in some sense "in" the world or constitutive of it. Now this is surely wrong, and Demos was right to point this out. A negative fact is not a fact which *exists* as positive facts do. Therefore, we may say that the world does not *consist* of positive and negative facts lying "side by side" as Russell implies. Russell's errors are avoided also by Wittgenstein's definition of a negative fact, to which we must now turn.

We also call the existence of states of affairs a positive fact, and their non-existence a negative fact. (2.06)

Here Wittgenstein makes it clear that a negative fact is not something existent in itself (like a positive fact) but merely the *absence or non-existence* of a positive fact. *A negative fact is a fact that does not exist, not an existent fact with the "property" of negativity.* In short, Wittgenstein's theory preserves the virtues of Demos' in that it too does not assert the *existence* of negative facts alongside positive ones, yet it escapes one of its basic defects, in that, by means of the notion of a negative fact Wittgenstein is able to show how a proposition can have one and only one negation. This is necessary for his radical logical and ontological pluralism, and cannot be supplied by Demos' theory.

Perhaps a possible *source* of Russell's view lies in the influence of Frege on his earlier doctrines. Russell seems to think of the proposition as a *name*, hence a true negative proposition describes or "names" an existing negative fact, which negative fact exists because of the existence of the negative proposition itself, just as the existence of the bearer of a name is presupposed by that name.

[31] *Ibid.*, p. 214.

Also, Russell's view would seem to imply that "not" is a name, and that there exist "logical objects", among them that denoted by "not". It is in cases like this that we can see the great merit of Wittgenstein's position, which clearly distinguishes between names and propositions.

We may now define what Wittgenstein means by a negative fact: a negative fact is the non-existence of a state of affairs, which non-existence is the one and only one fact which negates (i.e., contradicts) that state of affairs. Wittgenstein's analogy (quoted above) also confirms this interpretation.

To the fact that a point is black there corresponds [*entspricht*] a positive fact, and to the fact that a point is white (not black), a negative fact. (4.063)

Thus, a positive fact (or facts) *corresponds* to a negative fact, and is *not equivalent to it* as in Demos.

A couple of remarks from the *Notebooks* will help further to explain Wittgenstein's position, especially his opposition to a view like Russell's.

The question here is: Is the positive fact primary, the negative secondary, or are they on the same level. And if so, how is it with the facts p V q, p⊃q, etc. Aren't these on the same level as -p? But then *must* not *all facts* be on the same level? The question is really this: Are there facts beside the positive ones? (For it is difficult not to confuse what is not the case with what *is* the case instead of it.)[32]

"What is not the case" is equivalent to the negative fact, and "what *is* the case instead of it" is the existence of a positive fact which is incompatible with (contrary to) the given fact. The point is that the former and the latter are not *identical*. Since the negative fact is merely the non-existence of a positive fact we can say that whenever a negative fact occurs it is *replaced* by a positive one, in the sense that a positive fact is always found existing in the "logical space" left open by the negative fact. (Thus, when a point is not-black, it is white.) Demos' error lay in confusing the former with the latter, and trying to identify one with the other.

[32] Wittgenstein, *op. cit.*, pp. 32e-33e.

If all the positive statements about a thing are made, aren't all the negative ones made too? And that is the whole point.[33]

In conclusion, I believe it is justifiable to claim that the following points have been established. (1) Negative facts are necessary for Wittgenstein because only by means of them can the total independence of elementary propositions and states of affairs be maintained. (2) Thus, elementary propositions can exclude, but not contradict, one another. (3) This latter condition makes it clear that an elementary proposition can have one and only one negation. (4) A negative fact is *defined* by Wittgenstein as the non-existence of a state of affairs. (5) This definition makes it possible to see that the doctrine of negative facts is really nothing more than the explanation of *how* an elementary proposition can have only one negation. And this was the main purpose of this chapter, namely, to show that a negative fact *is* the single negation of an elementary proposition. I will now turn to my discussion of Wittgenstein's theory of truth and falsehood.

[33] *Ibid.*, p. 33e.

VI

TRUTH AND FALSEHOOD

> What a picture represents is its sense. (2.221)
>
> The agreement or disagreement of its sense with reality constitutes its truth or falsity (2.222)

In this chapter I would like to discuss what I believe are the basic features of Wittgenstein's theory of truth and falsehood. My exposition will be concerned primarily with establishing the following four views. (1) Every genuine proposition can be denied, i.e., every significant proposition can be true *or* false. A corollary to this is that tautologies and contradictions are not genuine propositions but rather their *limits*. This will be illustrated by a brief sketch of Wittgenstein's notion of the general form of proposition. (2) We know the sense of a proposition if we know what would be the case *if* it were true. This establishes the close relationship between sense and truth in Wittgenstein's thought. I will briefly contrast the latter's view on this question with Strawson's and Frege's. (3) A proposition and its denial (i.e., p and -p) refer to the *same fact* but have *opposite senses*. The understanding of this view should be greatly facilitated by what was said in the last chapter. Here it will be found that negation exists only in language (which is really only another way of expressing (3)). (4) Finally, I will discuss the general *conditions* under which we are justified in holding a given proposition to be true. These conditions will be seen to constitute what is generally called the "correspondence" theory of truth, that is, the view that a proposition is true if it agrees with non-linguistic reality. However, I hope to point out that Wittgenstein's position differs in some respects from traditional formulations of this theory, in that there are no psychological or empirical elements in his view. Also, it will be seen that the "agreement" of the proposition with reality is neither a relation nor a property. But before beginning my exposition proper there are a couple of preliminary remarks I wish to make.

First, although in the following discussion I will constantly refer to Wittgenstein's "theory" of truth, strictly speaking this locution is inaccurate. Wittgenstein does not have a "theory" of truth for the same reasons he does not have a "theory" of meaning (see Chapter IV). It will be seen at the end of this chapter that, since truth is not a thing, fact, property, or relation, it is not something we can have a theory *about*. In other words, it is not something "objective" in the world waiting to be "grasped" or "known". Truth is simply the "agreement" of the sense of a proposition with an existent state of affairs. What this "agreement" ultimately consists of is not a fact and hence cannot be the subject-matter of a theory. It is merely shown (*gezeigt*) or reflected as the *result* of our act of comparing the sense of the proposition with reality. Wittgenstein's remarks on this subject are not, then, aimed at giving us a theory to explain this, but merely at helping us to *see* it. Once again we are led to Wittgenstein's conception of philosophy as an activity, and not a doctrine (4.112, 6.54). This should become clearer as we proceed.

Second, in my discussion of Wittgenstein's views on truth and falsity I will restrict myself entirely to the truth and falsity of *elementary* propositions. These form the basis of Wittgenstein's theory of truth, as they do of his theory of meaning. Wittgenstein's doctrine of elementary propositions and states of affairs, in addition to the view that the logical constants are operations and not names of existent entities, allows him to assert that *both* the meaning and truth of all non-elementary propositions is dependent upon and derivative from that of their elementary constituents. In short, all propositions (*Sätze*) are truth-functions of their constituent elementary propositions.

I will begin by considering one of the most fundamental aspects of Wittgenstein's theory of truth and falsehood, namely, the view that every genuine proposition can be either true or false; or, in other words, every genuine proposition has a significant denial.

What a picture represents it represents independently of its truth or falsity, by means of its pictorial form. (2.22)

In an earlier discussion of logical space (Chapter V) we saw that every significant proposition occupies a single logical place in that space (2.202), just as every physical body occupies a single place in physical space. In addition, the proposition reaches through the whole of logical space (3.42) in the sense that it, together with its denial, encompasses the whole of logical space.

Now, when Wittgenstein says a proportion "reaches through" the whole of logical space he is referring to the possibility of its being either true *or* false, or of its being significantly denied. Thus, a "proposition" that was (say) *necessarily* true or false could not be significantly denied. In fact, it could not be a genuine proposition, i.e., a picture of the world, at all. Such a necessary "proposition" would, for Wittgenstein, be either a tautology (if it were necessarily true) or a contradiction (if it were necessarily false) (4.464). A proposition that is necessarily true (e.g., p & -p) leaves *open* the whole of logical space, whereas one that is necessarily false *fills* the whole of logical space. Neither alternative permits the proposition to occupy a *place* in logical space, but rather each *limits* it from opposite "directions" (4.463).

For instance, if p occupies a place in logical space, and -p all the places that lie outside the one filled by p, the whole is occupied by p and -p together. However, if we assert the tautology -(p & -p) then no (one) place in logical space is being referred to or pictured, for what a tautology asserts is that *every* place is empty. It is consistent with all possible state of affairs in the world, and being consistent with all it describes none (4.462). The converse is true for contradiction. A contradiction (p & -p) cannot occupy a place in logical space nor describe a possible state of affairs because it denies that *any* state of affairs could possibly fit it. Neither tautology nor contradiction picture anything in the world because everything in the world could be otherwise than it is. And since they do not picture the world they lack sense (*Sinn*) and are hence pseudo-propositions (4.461). In short, a necessary "proposition" is not a proposition at all.[1] To be a genuine proposition it must be capable of being true *or* false.

The above can be seen from another point of view. For Wittgenstein, all non-elementary propositions are truth-functions of elementary propositions, the latter being truth-functions of themselves. The former thus can be all derived from the latter by the successive application of a single operation, the stroke-function (symbolized as "/"), or joint denial.

Since *all* propositions can be generated by means of the repeated application of this operation we have in effect a general *description* of all propositions, or what Wittgenstein calls the "general form of propositions", or the "general form of a truth-function": $[(\bar{p}, \bar{\xi}, N(\bar{\xi})]$. "p" represents a given elementary proposition; "ξ" is the class of all elementary propositions; "N" is the operation of denial; and "-" designates that the class as a *whole* is referred to. Thus, the expression reads: for any given elementary proposition ($\bar{p}$) and for all elementary propositions ($\bar{\xi}$) we can apply the operation of denial (N) to the latter ($\bar{\xi}$) thereby deriving all possible propositions (*Sätze*) (Cite 5.47ff.). Thus, all non-elementary propositions are generated by using a given set of elementary propositions as *bases* for the application of the operation of denial, the *results* of which application can in turn be used as bases, either by themselves or in conjunction with the original bases. (Of course, if our operation results in a tautology this cannot be used as the *base* of a subsequent operation, since a tautology cannot be denied. The tautology signifies that we have reached the *limit* of our operation, and must either stop altogether or find different propositions for bases.) This operation can be continuously applied to any *finite* number of elementary propositions until, by a kind of process of elimination, the whole range of significant propositions, from tautology at one end to contradiction at the other, can be derived. (Strictly speaking, tautology and contradiction are not *included* in the list of derived propositions since they are not genuine propositions. Rather, they are the *limits* of that list.) The *number* of these derived

[1] In addition, a proposition's *certainty* or *impossibility* is defined by whether or not it is a tautology or a contradiction (respectively) (5.525).

propositions is determined by the formula $t^{(t^p)}$: "t" represents the number of truth-values, and "p" is the number of propositions. Thus, for two truth-values (truth and falsity) and two elementary propositions, the formula is $2^{(2^2)}$, or 16. It will be remembered that the number of *rows* for the truth-table is determined by the formula: t^p. The t has to be *repeated* in the formula for the number of derived propositions, for there we are not just concerned with finding the number of *rows* but with finding *all* the possible truth-combinations. (The latter is analogous to finding the *area* of a plane figure, and the former to finding its circumference.)

Now, the general form of proposition, in being a description of how all propositions can be derived from a given finite class of elementary propositions, presupposes that these elementary propositions *can* be denied. If a given proposition could *not* be significantly denied it would not fit the general form of proposition, and hence, would not be a proposition at all. To be a proposition a sentence must fit the general form of proposition, and to fit the general form of proposition it must be capable of being denied, i.e., of being true or false. The application of the stroke-function to a proposition p (p/p) yields -p. If -p were *not* possible, then the stroke could not be applied to p, and vice versa. This in turn means that p can *not* be substitued for $\bar{p}$ and ξ in $[\bar{p}, \xi, N(\bar{\xi})]$, which entails that p is not a proposition.

The consequence of the two arguments above is that so-called "necessary propositions" are not genuine propositions. At worst they are nonsensical (*unsinnig*), and at best they are tautologies, in which case they are senseless (*sinnlos*) and tell us nothing about the world. This principle, if it is true, is of great importance to philosophy. For here Wittgenstein has rejected the whole "quest for certainty" that has characterized (or perhaps plagued) all of modern philosophy since Descartes. Wittgenstein's general form of proposition and his doctrine that the *only* significant propositions are those which can be true *or* false, has rendered the quest for the indubitable proposition which is to serve as the basis and starting point of all philosophizing a quest for a chimera.[2] The goal of

[2] I do not mean to imply that all indubitable propositions are necessary,

this quest, if attained, would be a senseless tautology, that is, no proposition at all. If we are to discover anything about the world, and if we are to talk meaningfully, we must abandon all so-called *a priori* truths and self-evident propositions. The price for certainty in these cases is high, for it may be had only at the cost of significant language and sense. We may add to this that to define genuine *knowledge* on the basis of the certainty of what is known also results in surrendering significance and sense. On this view, since the only propositions which are necessarily true are tautologies the only propositions we can be said to *know* are tautologies. But then what we "know" has no sense, and hence it is vacuous to talk of "knowing" it.

'A knows that *p* is the case', has no sense [*sinnlos*] if *p* is a tautology. (5.1362)

The trouble with saying *I know* p when p is necessary is that it looks as if we are asserting a *logical connection* between our knowing and p. Also, it implies that p as a *symbol* is the *object* of our knowing. This is a mistake. Such cases fall into the same class of judgments as "A says p", "A believes p", and hence they too are correctly analyzed into "'p' says p" (5.541). This analysis shows that the propositional *sign* only, not the symbol, is involved. Propositions as symbols or pictures are not the *objects* of believing, saying, knowing or thinking.

A corollary to Wittgenstein's denial that a significant proposition may be one which is necessarily true is the following:

To understand a proposition means to know what is the case if it is true. (One can understand it, therefore, without knowing whether it is true.)

It is understood by anyone who understands its constituents [i.e., its names]. (4.024)

Here Wittgenstein is saying that our understanding of the sense of a proposition does not depend on the actual truth of that proposition. In our discussion of meaning we saw that the sense of a

---

i.e., that there are no contignent indubitable propositions. Here, I am concerned with those philosophers who, when distinguishing between indubitability and necessity, *grounded* the former in the latter.

proposition is not anything actual — not a fact or thing — but rather the possibility expressed by its pictorial form. Now we are in a position to add to this that what the pictorial form expresses is the possibility of a proposition's being true or false. For, since a picture by virtue of its pictorial form pictures reality by representing the possibility of the existence and non-existence of states of affairs (2.201), and the truth of an elementary proposition is determined by whether the state of affairs it pictures exists (4.25), we can conclude that the sense of a picture is dependent upon its *truth-conditions*. That is, in order to understand a proposition's sense we must know what would be the case *if* it were true (4.024 above). Thus, sense and truth are intimately related, but we must keep in mind that Wittgenstein is not talking about *actual* truth. He is not saying that we can only understand the sense of a proposition if we know that it is *actually* true. Indeed, the latter case is the complete antithesis of Wittgenstein's view, though it is central to any philosophical view which holds, for example, that we can know the sense of sense-data statements *because* their referents, the sense-data, are immediately present to us and determining their actual truth.

Wittgenstein's position on the relationship between sense and truth can be clarified by contrasting him with Frege and Strawson. For Frege,[3] a proposition is a "name" and has both *Sinn* (sense) and *Bedeutung* (reference). The *Bedeutung* of a proposition is the True or the False, the latter determining respectively the actual truth or falsity of the proposition. A proposition without a *Bedeutung* is therefore neither true nor false, though it can have *Sinn*. (It would lack *Sinn* only if its constituent names had no reference.) For Strawson[4] also a proposition can have meaning independent of its truth or falsity, for the sense of a sentence does not itself guarantee that an *assertion* (or genuine statement)

[3] Cf. Gottlob Frege, "On Sense and Reference", in *Translations From the Philosophical Writings of Gottlob Frege*, ed. by P. Geach and M. Black (Oxford, Basil Blackwell, 1960), pp. 56-79.

[4] P. F. Strawson, "On Referring", *Essays in Conceptual Analysis*, ed. by Antony Flew (London, MacMillan & Co. Ltd., 1960), pp. 21-52.

has been made. We can merely "consider" a sentence as (say) a linguistic entity and not assert it, i.e., not *use* it as a statement to express something true or false. But in either case the sentence has meaning.[5] For Wittgenstein, however, although the sense of a proposition is not dependent on its *actual* truth it is dependent on the *possibility* of its truth.

> We know its sense, if we know in what circumstances it *could* be used to make a statement.[6]

Frege's divorce of sense and truth goes hand in hand with his notion of assertion. For him, a proposition does not assert *itself*; *we* assert it. Frege devised a symbol to express this which he called the "assertion sign" (⊢).[7] Hence, an asserted as opposed to unasserted proposition had "⊢" prefixed to it. ⊢ p could thus be true or false; p could not be, although it had *Sinn*.[8] The assertion sign thus allows us to pass from the proposition to reality (the True and the False), and this "passing" Frege defined as judgment.

Wittgenstein wholly rejected this doctrine, for it implied that a proposition could assert of *itself* that it is in fact true. For Wittgenstein, what the presence of "⊢" before a proposition signified was merely that the person who wrote it there (e.g., Frege himself) happened to believe it to be true (4.442). A proposition does not assert of itself that it is *actually* true. Rather,

> A proposition shows how things stand *if* it is true. And it *says that* [*sagt*] they do so stand. (4.022)

The proposition shows its truth-conditions via its sense and pictorial

[5] As Anscombe points out, neither Frege nor Strawson completely *divorce* meaning and truth. They merely hold that a proposition does not *say* anything true or false if its truth-conditions have not actually been determined. G. E. M. Anscombe, *An Introduction to Wittgenstein's Tractatus* (London, Hutchinson University Library, 1959), p. 60. This still puts them in contrast with Wittgenstein, however, who denies that one can "consider" a proposition apart from its possible truth or falsity.

[6] *Ibid.*, p. 57.

[7] Frege, *op. cit.*, p. 1 ff.

[8] Something serving the same function as Frege's assertion sign is, I think, built into Strawson's view.

form, and says that such-and-such is the case via its own intrinsic nature; we do not have to add a ⊢ to it to make it do this (4.064). A proposition is *always* asserted as being true or false. If this were not so, then in order to understand the *sense* of a proposition we would have to know whether it is to be thought of as something true or false, and this leads to an infinite regress.[9]

We have seen that it is the essence of a proposition to be true or false. We can express this by saying that every proposition has T-F poles, and by writing a given proposition p as "T p F" we bring this out (6.1203). Thus, Wittgenstein compares propositions to arrows (3.144),[10] in that their sense "points out" a region of logical space. This means that every proposition asserts the *same* fact regardless of whether it is true or false; or in other words, p and -p *both refer to the same fact.* That is, the same fact makes both p true and -p false, or vice versa. The possibility of p and -p having opposite senses but being determined as true or false by the same fact is grounded in Wittgenstein's view of negation.

> But it is important that the signs '*p*' and '*-p*' *can* say the same thing. For it shows that nothing in reality corresponds to the sign '-'.
>
> The occurrence of negation in a proposition is not enough to characterize its sense (*--p* = *p*).
>
> The propositions '*p*' and '*-p*' have opposite sense, but there corresponds to them one and the same reality. (4.0621)

The view that p and -p have opposite senses (*Sinne*) yet refer to the same reality or fact can easily lead to confusion, for it seems at first that p and -p must refer to *different* facts. For example, let p be the proposition "It is raining". If I assert p I am talking about the rain. But if I *deny* p, and say "It is not raining", *this* (it may be said) is not about the rain at all, but about something else (e.g., that it is sunny, or snowing). Thus, the argument runs, p and -p are *about* different facts, and are not pictures of the *same*

[9] Alexander P. Maslow, *A Study of Ludwig Wittgenstein's Tractatus Logico-Philosophicus* (Berkeley, Cal., University of California Press, 1961), p. 77.

[10] In the same passage (3.144) Wittgenstein compares names to points, thus illustrating the sharpest contrast between names and propositions. Here we see how far Frege's *Sinn* has come in the hands of Wittgenstein.

fact, because when we deny p we get a different proposition, -p, If p is "It is raining", then if p is true I know *both* that it is raining and that it is not (say) snowing. Thus it seems that p and -p are about different facts after all, p being about the rain and -p being about (say) the snow.

The above view is mistaken as far as Wittgenstein's own account is concerned. To see why this is so let us recall Wittgenstein's conception of a negative fact as the one and only one significant negation of a proposition. The negation of p ("It is raining") is -p ("It is not raining"), not the assertion of some *other* proposition, e.g., "It is snowing", or "It is sunny". For the latter, though *incompatible* with p, do not *contradict* it, i.e., are not equivalent to -p. *A false proposition is not false because something else is true; it is false because its denial is true.* The same reality (fact) corresponds to p and -p because, not being able to be true and false at the same time, the fact that shows p to be true *automatically* shows -p to be false and vice versa. To say that p refers to one fact and -p to another implies (1) that *both* could be true at the same time, i.e., that both could assert true propositions though about different facts. (In our example, p asserted the fact that it is raining, and -p the fact that it is snowing, or sunny, etc.) But this is obviously not the right explanation, because p & -p is a contradiction, and also because the assertion of *different facts* cannot be equivalent to the negation of p. It also assumes (2) that denial adds to the *sense* of a proposition. That is, to negate p changes p into a different proposition with a different sense (e.g., q). But "-" is not a *name*; there are no "logical objects" which it designates (4.0621). This is easily seen by a consideration of double negation. When we negate -p we get --p, which is equivalent to p. This is never the case for names. When we repeat a name we do not "cancel it out". We might say that we are emphasizing it, or calling attention to it; at worst we would be merely redundant. Negation is not a *property* either. As we saw earlier, there are no negative facts in the sense of an existent fact with the property of being-negative. Negation is merely a logical *operation* and in no way characterizes the actual *sense* of a proposition. "If 'not' were an existent quality like red, then it would be impossible for p to say either f or -f",[11] i.e., to say what is the case *and* what is not the case.

In 4.061 and 4.062 Wittgenstein suggests that, since the sense of a proposition is independent of what is the case, we might *reverse* the meanings of p and -p, so that -p meant p and p meant -p.

In that case one could say, for example, that '*p*' signified in the true way what '-*p*' signified in the false way, etc. (4.061)

Can we not make ourselves understood with false propositions, just as we have done up till now with true ones? — So long as it is known that they are meant to be false. (4.062)

Wittgenstein gives a peremptory "No!" to this suggestion, because such a change would not affect the *meanings* of p and -p. When we assert a proposition we say that something is the case, and if by -p we meant p, and -p happens to be true, then we have merely said what p said *before* the change. Negation and the negation-sign still retain their meanings, "... and this is enough to show that 'not' itself has nothing corresponding to it in reality:[12] its presence does not determine the sense of a proposition."[13]

Propositions, as well as facts, are essentially positive, since only positive facts *exist*. The *same* picture can say both what is the case and what is not the case. If we were to picture what is *not* the case we would merely picture some *other* fact that *is* the case instead of it. We cannot *picture* something *not*-existing.[14]

If a picture presents what-is-not-the-case in the forementioned way, this only happens through its representing *that* which *is* not the case.

For the picture says, as it were: '*This* is how it is *not*,' and to the question '*How* is it not?' just the positive proposition is the answer.[15]

[11] G. D. O'Brien, *Meaning and Fact: A Study in the Philosophy of Wittgenstein.* Unpublished doctoral dissertation, University of Chicago, 1960, p. 36.

[12] When negating p we could merely turn it upside down, i.e., write b, instead of writing -p. This device would make it clear that the negation-sign does not add to the *sense* of the negated proposition, and that p and -p refer to the same fact. (I am indebted to Prof. Henry W. Johnstone, Jr. for this suggestion).

[13] Anscombe, *op. cit.*, p. 77.

[14] *Ibid.*, pp. 69-70.

[15] Ludwig Wittgenstein, *Notebooks 1914-1916*, ed. by G. E. M. Anscombe and G. H. von Wright (Oxford, Basil Blackwell, 1961), p. 25e.

Negation exists only in language. To illustrate this, consider the following diagram which Wittgenstein uses in the *Notebooks.*[16]

That two people are not fighting can be represented by representing them as not fighting and also by representing them as fighting and saying that the picture shows how things are *not.*[17]

Thus, there can be *two* ways of expressing a negative fact (e.g., that two people are not fighting) by means of the *same* picture.[18]

(1) We can show a picture of them fighting (as the diagram above does), and then negate it.
(2) We can show a picture of them doing something else, e.g., shaking hands.

But in *both* cases negation is only in the language. Both the facts pictured are positive in nature.

We can now see the general grounds or conditions for the truth or falsity of a given elementary proposition.

What a picture represents is its truth or falsity. (2.221)
The agreement or disagreement of its sense [*Sinn*] with reality [*Wirklichkeit*] constitutes its truth or falsity. (2.222)
In order to tell whether a picture is true or false we must compare it with reality. (2.223)

The view that the truth or falsity of a proposition is determined (respectively) by its agreement or disagreement with non-linguistic reality is what is traditionally called the correspondence theory of truth: a proposition (or "thought") is true if it corresponds to or agrees with reality, and false otherwise. Wittgenstein's position may be classified in terms of this theory *if* one keeps in mind that

16 *Ibid.*, p. 7.
17 *Ibid.*, p. 23.
18 Strictly speaking, of course, we cannot negate an ordinary picture, only proposition-pictures. The use of the diagram by Wittgenstein is not meant to imply this, for it is intended as an illustration of a proposition-picture.

there are no empirical or psychological factors involved. A psychological conception of the correspondence theory would hold, for example, that a statement is true if and only if it refers to a mental thought (e.g., an image) which in turn is a "copy" of some actual state of affairs in the world. Thus, the statement "The cat is on the mat" is true if and only if it refers to a mental image (which, of course, is a mental *fact*) of a cat on a mat, which in turn is a copy of the actual state of affairs cat-being-on-the-mat. For Wittgenstein, however, all psychological factors such as the above are excluded. What he means by a picture (*Bild*) has nothing to do with *mental* "pictures" (images). (See Chapter III). In this Wittgenstein follows his analysis of meaning, where he also rigorously excluded all psychological factors. For Wittgenstein, the introduction of psychology would make his theory epistemological, but epistemology, due to its relation to psychology, plays no part in logic or philosophy (4.1121).

As Ramsey pointed out, Wittgenstein has reduced the problem of the analysis of *judgment* (which always involves something psychological or empirical) to the question, "What is it for a proposition-token to have a certain sense?"[19] And since the latter question is purely logical, psychology is ruled out. The major proof of this reduction for Ramsey is Wittgenstein's analysis of intensional statements such as "A says p", or "A believes p", where A is a person and p is a proposition-symbol (Cf. 5.541). The problem raised by such statements is that they seem to show that a proposition can occur in a context other than that of being a truth-functional constituent of another proposition. That is, it seems that such statements can be true or false *independent* of the truth or falsity of the proposition p which occurs in them. They also presuppose that a proposition as a *symbol* can be the *object* of a mental attitude or a *content* of a mind. This, if true, would introduce an empirical and psychological element into logic and theory of meaning, as well as undermine the allegedly universal

[19] F. P. Ramsey, *The Foundations of Mathematics* (Paterson, New Jersey, Littlefield, Adams & Co., 1960), p. 275.

truth-functional nature of language. Wittgenstein denies all this by showing that the apparent form of such intensional propositions is not their real form, and that a proper analysis of intensional statements reveals that the proposition as a symbol (i.e., as a proposition proper) does not occur as a *constituent.* Rather, only the *sign* of the proposition is involved. Hence, the analysis of "A says p" is: "'p' says p" (5.542). Here, both the proposition as symbol and the "person" or "subject" disappear; all that remains is a proposition-sign asserting a proposition. But this says ultimately nothing more than the proposition *itself,* since the sign of a proposition is shown be merely writing the proposition itself.

Psychology entered into Frege's theory via the view that an unasserted proposition could have sense (*Sinn*) independent of its truth-value. It was the business of judgment to assert the proposition, i.e., give it a truth-value, which assertion is expressed by the sign "⊢". Judgment enables us to pass from the sentence to non-linguistic reality, the True and the False.[20] But since for Wittgenstein a proposition's sense cannot be independent of the *possibility* of its being true or false (4.022) the role that judgment plays in Frege is rendered superfluous and irrelevant.

In addition to excluding all psychological factors such as those involved in belief and judgment, Wittgenstein's theory of truth excluded everything *empirical,* even in the broadest sense. Because of this he is not talking about *verification.* Wittgenstein does give us the necessary conditions which justify our assertion that a given proposition is true, but this is *not* the same thing as telling us how we should actually go about determining the truth of a given proposition. The latter is implicit in the notion of verification, for it includes references to the methods or *rules* by which propositions are shown to be true or false, i.e., verified. In order to give such rules, however, we must resort to considering particular cases. This is ruled out for Wittgenstein on general grounds because it is an empirical matter (and hence irrelevant to logic), and also because he does not give us any particular *examples* of

[20] Frege, "On Sense and Reference", *op. cit.*, pp. 63-65.

elementary propositions which could serve as cases to be verified. The giving of particular examples of elementary propositions would probably be the business of psychology.

Keeping the above qualifications in mind, then, I think we may justifiably say that Wittgenstein's theory of truth and falsity is basically an expression of the traditional correspondence theory. A proposition is true if and only if it agrees with reality, and false otherwise.

If an elementary proposition is true, the state of affairs [*Sachverhalt*] exists: if an elementary proposition is false, the state of affairs does not exist. (4.25)

If p is an elementary proposition then we may say: (1) p is true if the state of affairs it pictures exists; p is false if the state of affairs it pictures does not exist. And conversely (2) -p is true if the state of affairs p pictures does not exist, -p is false if the state of affairs p pictures exists. What determines the truth or falsity of an elementary proposition (positive or negative) is simply whether the state of affairs its sense pictures exists or does not exist.

Thus, p is not false because, e.g., it pictures the existence of some *other* state of affairs; a false proposition is not a true proposition about something else. Also, a negative proposition (-p) is true when the state of affairs p describes does not exist, i.e., when some other state of affairs exists (though it is not specified which). But it must be remembered that although, when -p is true, some state of affairs *other* than that described by p exists, the existence of this other state of affairs is not the *reason* for the truth of -p — it is not *why* -p is true. The reason why -p is true is simply that p is false, i.e., the fact p describes does not exist. Also it follows that -p is not true because it describes an existent state of affairs with the property of negativity. "-" does not characterize a propositions's sense (4.0621); there is no property of "negativeness" in a state of affairs because "-" is not a name. All states of affairs are positive in content. Negation exists only in the realm of language — *we* negate propositions — it is an *operation* we perform on propositions.

There is one more important point that must be discussed in regard to Wittgenstein's position on truth and falsity. Although a proposition is true if it agrees with reality such agreement (or correspondence) should not be thought of as (1) a *relation* the proposition has to reality, nor (2) as an object or property. (1) An elementary proposition is true if the state of affairs it describes exists, and false otherwise (4.25). In other words, it is not true because it is *related* to that state of affairs by the relation of "agreement". Truth is the *result* of the act of comparing a proposition with reality and seeing that it does agree. The "agreement" is simply an expression of the success of this application. It is not some entity or relation that can be described or asserted by a proposition, and hence cannot be the constituent of a proposition. That a proposition is true shows (*zeigt*) itself in and through the proposition's agreeing with reality. Conversely, the falsehood of a proposition is not a relation that a proposition has to some fact other than the one it asserts. Falsehood is not a *kind* of correspondence, but the *lack* of any correspondence.

> The falsehood of the proposition is not due to another and independent relation of correspondence between the proposition and the fact.
>
> Falsehood is simply a lack or absence of correspondence, is noncorrespondence between the proposition and the facts: ... it is a failure of the truth claim of the proposition to be justified by the state of affairs, and not a justification of the impossible claim.[21]

True and false are not "relations of equal status between signs and what they signify" (4.061).

(2) True and false are also not *objects* or *properties*. The words "true" and "false" are not names of things or of any constituents of a fact. When we say that a sentence is true we are not using "true" to designate some property in the fact (its "truth") that *makes* it true. The same holds, of course, for falsehood.

> ... But if a proposition has no sense, nothing corresponds to it, since it does not designate a thing (a truth-value) which might have properties called 'false' or 'true'. The verb of a proposition is not 'is true' or 'is

[21] Maslow, *op. cit.*, p. 78.

false', as Frege thought: rather, that which 'is true' must already contain the verb. (4.063)

This is, of course, a radical rejection of Frege's doctrine of the True and the False as being the ultimate referents of propositions, and as being that which determines their truth or falsity. To say that a proposition is true, i.e., to say "p is true", is merely to assert that proposition. Hence, p is true ≡ p.

I will now conclude with a summary of the major aspects of Wittgenstein's theory of truth and falsehood brought out in this chapter. (1) Every significant proposition can be true or false. This is expressed by the general form of proposition (which presupposes the possibility of a proposition's denial) and by the view that tautology and contradiction are not significant propositions themselves, but rather the limits of significant propositions. (2) The relation between sense and truth is that we know the sense of a proposition if we know what would be the case *if* it were true. Sense ultimately has reference to a range of possibility, not an actuality. (3) Negation exists only in language; p and -p refer to the same fact although they have opposite senses. (This was also seen in Chapter V, where negative facts were defined as non-existent facts, not as existent ones with the property of negativity.) (4) The general condition for holding a proposition to be true is therefore the following: a proposition is true if the state of affairs it describes (pictures) exists, and is false if it does not exist. This basically coincides with what is traditionally called the correspondence theory of truth. Wittgenstein may therefore be said to held the latter if it is divested of all psychological and empirical elements. Also, we saw that truth is not a relation or property.

Finally, I would like to point out that Wittgenstein's theory of meaning adds a necessary element to the correspondence theory of truth, which many other formulations cannot, or do not, supply. This additional element is found at the heart of Wittgenstein's picture theory of meaning, namely, the notion of logical form. The latter constitutes the possibility of a logical isomorphism of structure between picture and fact. When this isomorphism is *actual* and the fact pictured exists we can say that the picture *agrees* with the fact. This agreement in turn determines that the proposition is *true*. (Here it should be clear that isomorphism and agreement are not identical, since the former has reference to possibility and the latter to actuality.) Thus, we may say that Wittgenstein's picture theory of meaning, seen in terms of the correspondence theory of truth, tries to answer the following question: How is it *possible* for a proposition to agree with (correspond to) reality? The answer is, on the one hand, because the proposition is a *picture* of reality, and on the other, because reality is nothing else than the referent of a proposition, i.e., a *fact*. Many philosophers "define" truth as the "agreement" of a proposition with reality, but they do not show how such an agreement is *possible*. It is one of the great virtues of Wittgenstein's picture theory of meaning that it attempts to do so.

CONCLUSION

I now wish to make my concluding remarks. I will begin by reminding the reader of those aspects of my general interpretation of the *Tractatus* which seem most important (Section A). I will then try to present an interpretation of Wittgenstein's final conclusions by focusing upon his views on philosophy, solipsism, the mystical and the notion of the world as a limited whole (Section B). Finally, I will offer a general criticism of the *Tractatus* directed at Wittgenstein's conception of the nature and aim of philosophy (Section C).

(A). First, in regard to Wittgenstein's *ontology*, I attempted to show the relationship between objects and facts, and see why Wittgenstein says the world is the totality of the latter and not of the former. I examined Wittgenstein's radical break with the tradition of reductive analysis, which break led to his separation of the simple in thought from the simple in reality, and the corollary view that only in and through complexity is significant discourse and a world possible. That is, although the object is logically simple it is not ontologically real, and although the state of affairs is logically complex it and only it can be held to constitute the world. Complex facts, not simple objects, are the constituents of the world and the objects of scientific knowledge. This conclusion also led to the realization that the nature of language determines that reality *is* what it can be *said* to be. Thus, the problem of ontology is ultimately identical with that of defining the nature of the object of science, since what the world is is coextensive with what can be known by science.

The exposition of the doctrine of names was expanded beyond the context of ontology to that of language. The proof that names are a necessary presupposition for the possibility of meaning (*Sinn*) was begun with a discussion of Russell's theory of descriptions. Because of the possibility of radical falsehood inherent in descriptions the latter constitute a limiting case or contrast by means of which it is seen that at least some propositions in our language must have logically proper names as constituents (a logically proper name being a simple term which always has a reference (*Bedeutung*)). At this point I began my exposition of the nature of elementary propositions, which are defined as consisting solely of names in immediate combination.

The first part of my exposition centered around three contentions: (1) objects are not sense-data; (2) elementary propositions are not sense-data statements (nor do they have the same function as the latter in theory of meaning); and (3) states of affairs are not simple sense-data but complex configurations of objects. Objects are the necessary conditions for the possibility of names, just as names are necessary conditions for the possibility of sense (*Sinn*). Objects are the eternal substance of the world and lack all material or empirical properties. They are both the constituents of states of affairs and the referents of names. The denial of the identity of elementary propositions and sense-data statements removes meaning from the realm of actuality and fact to that possibility. The real essence of the picture theory of meaning was asserted to lie in the notion of logical (*logische*) or pictorial form (*Form der Abbildung*), which all propositions *must* share with the facts they represent *if* they are to represent them. The sense (*Sinn*) of a proposition is therefore the realm of possibility — the area of logical space — which its logical form "describes" and makes possible. Since every proposition must share its logical form with the fact it pictures two further characteristics of pictures (*Bilder*) emerge: multiplicity and order. That is, the names of an elementary proposition must have both the same multiplicity and the same order as the objects of the fact it pictures. This in turn gives rise to the concept of the logical *isomorphism* of picture and fact. At this point I criticized some traditional attempts to undermine or deny this isomorphism, namely, those of Daitz, Stenius, and Evans.

I tried to show that their criticisms all rest on a mistaken assumption about the nature of an elementary proposition and the nature of relations. For example, their attempt to break down the isomorphism of picture and fact presupposes the possibility of treating relation-words as names and relations as objects. For Wittgenstein, however, this is a fundamental mistake. Once this is realized (and Wittgenstein's own position is fully understood) it becomes clear that such criticisms are irrelevant to the picture theory as formulated by him, and hence reflect a misunderstanding of that theory.

I concluded my discussion of Wittgenstein's theory of meaning with a further analysis of the nature of logical form, together with some of its consequences. It was argued that the most important of these are the distinction between saying and showing, and the mystical. The logical form of language is intrinsically and necessarily beyond the realm of any kind of description, since any attempt to articulate it presupposes that we can transcend the limits of language. And because such a transcendence is ultimately self-contradictory all attempts to construct a *theory* of the logical structure of language (for instance, Carnap's program of logical syntax) are doomed to failure. Thus, the essence of language, that by means of which it pictures the world, cannot itself be pictured by language, but can only be *shown.* This amounts to a denial of the possibility of a meta-language regress and a rejection of the traditional "third Man" argument. The consequence of this is the realization of the radical finitude of the world and of the mystical. There is no other meaningful (*sinnvoll*) linguistic function outside and beyond that of asserting the existence and non-existence of states of affairs. Finally, it was pointed out that the key to the solution of the "separation" of thought and reality is provided by the concept of logical form and the denial that meaning is grounded in actuality or fact.

Once we had found that all significant discourse is constructed out of the fact-stating function of elementary propositions only two major problems remained. These were (1) negation and negative facts, and (2) the nature of truth and falsehood. Problem (2) was defined as that of the determination of the general conditions which allow us to assert that a given proposition is true (or false). The solution of problem (1) took the form of defining a negative fact as *the* negation of an elementary proposition, it being necessary that an elementary proposition have one and only one denial (contradictory). This also avoids the difficulties in asserting the *existence* (or ontological reality) of negative facts. The theory of truth thus follows easily and naturally once the ground has been prepared for it in the theory of meaning. Truth is defined as the agreement of an elementary proposition with reality; or more exactly: an elementary proposition is true if and only if the state of affairs its sense represents exists. The final conclusion is the denial that truth is a *relation*, that is, that the agreement or correspondence a proposition has with reality is a relation that holds *between* the proposition and reality. Truth and falsehood are simply the *results* of the act of comparing propositions with facts. Thus, there is no "theory" of truth just as there is no "theory" of meaning.

(B). Truth and meaning are not *facts*, and it is only facts one can have theories *about*. Now, it is the business of science to formulate true propositions and theories about the facts, i.e., about the world.

The totality of true propositions is the whole of natural science (or the whole corpus of the natural sciences). (4.11)

But,

Philosophy is not one of the natural sciences. (4.111)

Philosophy is an activity (*Tätigkeit*), not a doctrine (*Lehre*). As such it aims at the logical clarification of thoughts and propositions. Moreover, these clarifications or elucidations (*Erläuterungen*) are not themselves propositions (4.112).

Philosophy settles controversies about the limits of natural science. (4.113)

It must set limits to what can be thought; and, in doing so, to what cannot be thought (4.114)

Now, the limits of thought can be set only from *within* the limits of the thinkable, that is, from within the limits of what can be *said*. But the limits of what can be said are the limits of *language*. And since the essence of language is determined by its logical form it is *logic* which sets the limits of language. Finally, the limits of language are the limits of the *world*. Thus, from the conception of philosophy as the activity of the logical analysis and clarification of thought, i.e., as setting the limits to what can be thought and said (4.112, 4.114), we arrive at the conclusion that the limits of language are identical with the limits of the world. Therefore, we may say that the activity of philosophy aims at setting the (logical) limits of the world.

But Wittgenstein is not content with merely asserting the ultimate identification of the limits of language and the world. He also says:

> *The limits of my language* mean the limits of my world. (5.6)

The use of the pronoun "my" to modify "language" and "world" implicitly introduces the notion of solipsism (*Solipsismus*). It emerges completely in the succeeding remarks where Wittgenstein identifies language with *my* language and world with *my* world, and the latter with the subject (*Subjekt*).

> Logic pervades the world: the limits of the world are also its limits.
> We cannot think what we cannot think; so what we cannot think we cannot *say* [*sagen*] either. (5.61)
>
> This remark provides the key to the problem, how much truth there is in solipsism.
> For what the solipsist *means* [*meint*] is quite correct; only it cannot be *said*, but makes itself manifest [*es zeigt sich*].
> The world is *my* world: this is manifest in the fact that the limits of language (of that language which alone I understand) mean the limits of *my* world. (5.62)

Wittgenstein's argument for solipsism can be summarized as follows:

(1) The limits of language are the limits of the subject (i.e., there is only *one* language I can understand).
(2) The limits of the world are the limits of language.

(3) Therefore, the limits of the world are the limits of the subject (i.e., the world is *my* world).

The crucial step towards solipsism is, of course, the major premise, where the limits of language are identified with those of the subject.[1] Once this step is admitted the conclusion (3) follows. Let us examine this in more detail.

The first thing that should be pointed out in trying to understand Wittgenstein's solipsism is that the world is not said to a content of the subject — it is not *in* the subject. Conversely, the subject cannot be said to "have" the world in itself, as for example, one "has" an idea in one's mind. To speak in this way implies an altogether illegitimate separation of the subject and the world such that they appear to be distinct and independent *entities*. Such a view holds that since all that exists are my Ego and its contents, so-called other Egos and their supposed contents do not exist. Everything exists as *object for me*, and my point of view or relation toward the world is the only one possible. Indeed, my point of view toward the world *is* the world. I suggest that this view arises first from the recognition of the truism that what I know *I* know (what I think *I* think, or what I experience *I* experience), and second from the belief that the I that knows is something over and above that which is known. The I (Ego) is then thought of as "beyond" the world and looking at it "from a distance" (as some people believe God does). These views, combined with a *substantial* conception of the I lead to the conclusion that the world is a *content* of the I. That is, the world belongs to, is an attribute of, the I. The world exists *for* me thus means the world exists *in* me.

It is possible to read the *Tractatus* and believe that Wittgenstein is a solipsist in something like the above sense. However, in light of other assertions in the *Tractatus* I think it becomes evident that Wittgenstein is definitely *not* a solipsist of this kind. What he means by solipsism is quite different from the traditional associations of that term and thus can be fully understood only within

[1] Cf. Jaako Hintikka, "On Wittgenstein's 'Solipsism'", *Mind*, LXVII, No. 265 (January 1958), pp. 88-91 *passim*. Hintikka calls this identification the "basis" of Wittgenstein's solipsism.

the context of the general doctrines of the *Tractatus* as a whole.
Following 5.62 (quoted above) Wittgenstein asserts that:

There is no such thing as the subject that thinks or entertains ideas. (5.631)

The subject for Wittgenstein is not a "thing" (e.g., a substance) that "has" ideas. The relation of the subject to the world may be illustrated by the concept of a circle in geometry. The subject limits the world just as the line forming the circumference of a circle limits the area of that circle. We cannot ask whether the circumference of a circle is "in" the circle — is part of its area — or is "outside" it — not a part of its area. The circumference, being a line and hence one-dimensional, is not a "thing" about which such questions can arise. It is merely a *limit* which functions as the determinant of the area of a circle. For Wittgenstein, the world is limited by the subject in the same way. The subject can neither be said to be inside (a part) of the world (as in materialism) nor outside it (as in some forms of idealism). Rather, the subject *is* the world.

The world is *my* world... . (5.62)

The subject, then, is always both "in" the world and "outside" the world in so far as it is neither the one nor the other. This paradox becomes a truism when properly understood. The subject can be seen from two aspects, depending on our point of view, just as the circumference of a circle can be seen from two aspects. That is, we can view the circumference either by looking *from* the center of the circle or by looking *toward* the center. In the former case the circumference is seen from the "inside", and in the latter case it is seen from the "outside". The circumference thus takes on two "dimensions" corresponding to each of these two points of view. In the same way, the subject takes on two "dimensions" depending on how we chose to view it. For Wittgenstein, the subject is the limit of the world and thus points *toward* the facts or the totality of existent states of affairs. But it is metaphysical in that it is not a fact *in* the world.

> The philosophical self [*Ich*] ... is the metaphysical subject, the limit of the world — not a part of it. (5. 641)

Thus, the subject also has an "aspect" pointing *away* from the world, or facts. (In Kantian terminology, we could say that these two "dimensions" of the subject correspond to the phenomenal and noumenal Egos.)

But for Wittgenstein we cannot *say* this. To attempt to do so would be to attempt to transcend the limits of language. All that language can describe are facts, and the subject, by its very nature, is not a fact. But *this* is just to say the subject is the *limit*. Any attempt to transcend the limits of language — say the unsayable, or think the unthinkable — is doomed to failure. We cannot stand outside the world and view it as a separate whole because we *are* that whole. The subject, as the limit of the world, always has the world "present" to it, though not in the sense that one may say of two distinct objects that one is *related* to the other. The latter notion presupposes that the *terms* of the relation could exist independent of the relation. But this is impossible if the "terms" involved are the subject and the world, since the subject is not a "thing" that could enter into a relation as a term. (So too, the circumference of a circle is not a "thing" that can be separated from the circle while at the same time the circle continues to exist, i.e., continues to have an area.) Thus, just as logic haunts our thinking, the subject haunts the world. The world is always present to a subject, and the subject always has the world present to it. In this regard, compare what Wittgenstein says a bit later about death, and the visual field.

> So too at death the world does not alter, but comes to an end. (6.431)
> Death is not an event [*Ereignis*] in life: we do not live to experience death [*Den Tod erlebt man nicht*].
>
> Our life has no end in just the way in which our visual field has no limits. (6.4311)

The last remark about the visual field refers back to 5.632-5.6331 where Wittgenstein uses this image to clarify the "relation" of the subject to the world. Given that the subject is a *limit* of the world he says:

Where *in* the world is a metaphysical subject to be found?
You will say that this is exactly like the case of the eye and the visual field. But really you do *not* see the eye.
And nothing *in the visual field* allows you to infer that it is seen by an eye. (5.633)

Just as the eye can see everything but itself, and everything that is seen is seen by the eye, so the subject can "see" everything but itself, and everything that is "seen" is "seen" by the subject. This, I think, is really a reformulation of Schopenhauer's idealism, which in turn is derived from Kant's transcendental idealism. For Schopenhauer, the world is my idea (*Vorstellung*) means that subject and object are mutual conditions for experience. They are distinct and irreducible, in that there can be no object without a subject and no subject without an object. In addition, the subject can never *become* an object, i.e., be known.[2]

But Wittgenstein goes even further beyond any form of idealism.

Here it can be seen that solipsism, when its implications are followed out strictly, coincides with pure realism. The self [*Ich*] of solipsism shrinks to a point without extension, and there remains the reality coordinated with it. (5.64)

Thus, for Wittgenstein, Schopenhauer's idealism — the world is my idea — and his own solipsism — the world is my world — both reduce to realism. This is simply to say that the self is "metaphysical", i.e., not a thing or fact. As Wittgenstein rather ironically expresses it, if one were to write a book entitled, *The World as I Found It*, no mention would be made therein of the subject (6.631). Moreover, although the doctrine of solipsism — or "pure realism" — cannot be expressed (*gesagt*) its truth is "manifest", i.e., it shows (*zeigt*) itself (5.62). This in turn is reminiscent of Kant's remark in the transcendental deduction of the first *Critique* that "it must be possible for the 'I think' to accompany all my representations". This proposition lies at the heart of Kant's

[2] Arthur Schopenhauer, *The World as Will and Representation*, trans. by E. F. J. Payne (Indian Hills, Colorado, Falcon's Wing Press, 1958), Vol. I, p. 3 ff. Cf. also G. E. M. Anscombe, *An Introduction to Wittgenstein's Tractatus* (London, Hutchinson University Library, 1959), pp. 161-175.

idealism and ultimately reduces to an identical proposition, i.e., one of the form: A = A.[3]

The "truth" of solipsism is thus a mere *truism*. The mistake of the traditional solipsist was that, although he came to Schopenhauer and Wittgenstein's insight that the world is my "idea" he thought one could infer from this my "idea" is the world. And although the latter is obviously false, for Wittgenstein the former, if properly understood, is obviously true. That solipsism is a "truism" is another way of saying that it and realism "coincide", that solipsism *reduces* to realism. But this is in turn grounded in the truth that the subject (Self, I) is not a thing, object or fact, but rather a metaphysical "extensionless point". Hence, the world — the totality of facts — does not include it as a constituent (5.631). We have seen that this conception of the world as the totality of facts is the core of Wittgenstein's ontology. I would now like to suggest that it, together with the coincidence of solipsism with realism, yields the further notion of the world as a limited whole (*begrenztes Ganz*), which is also the key to Wittgenstein's mysticism.[4]

> To view the world *sub specie aeterni* is to view it as a whole — a limited whole.
>
> Feeling the world as a limited whole — it is this that is mystical. (6.45)

For Wittgenstein, the world is not only a totality (*Gesamtheit*) of facts but this totality is also both limited and a whole. We may express the latter by saying that the world is radically *finite*, or more exactly, that it can be "viewed" as such. What does this mean?

First, it is clear that the finitude of the world — its being a limited whole — does *not* mean that only a finite number of facts constitute it. Rather, the world's finitude is grounded in the view that certain things "lie outside" (*liegen ausserhalb*) it. Thus, the

[3] Immanuel Kant, *Critique of Pure Reason*, 2nd ed., trans. by N. K. Smith (London, MacMillan & Co. Ltd., 1961), p. 152ff.

[4] The following remarks should be read with my discussion of the mystical in connection with the logical and pictorial form of language, in Chapter IV, in order to see how the notion of the world as a limited whole emerges from the theory of meaning.

world would be finite in this sense even if there were an infinite number of facts constituting it. What lies "outside" the world? Obviously, whatever is *not a fact*, since the world is simply identical with the totality of facts. But what does this include? On the basis of what has been said so far (Chapter IV) I think we may answer that logical and pictorial form lie outside the world.[5] This is implied by their not being facts, which in turn implies that they cannot be *expressed* by language (though of course all significant language presupposes them (4.121)). But logical form is also the *limit* of the world, which is identified with the subject (5.632 ff.). Hence, the subject is identical with the essence of language (solipsism). The subject too lies "outside" the world, i.e., is "metaphysical". And since logical form, as the essence of language, is the ground of its meaning (*Sinn*), we may say that all linguistic meaning lies "outside" the world. But in addition, *other* kinds of meaning lie outside the world, e.g., the sense of the world itself, and value.

The sense [*Sinn*] of the world must lie outside the world ... in it no value [*Wert*] exists — and if it did, it would have no value. (6.14)

And so it is impossible for there to be propositions of ethics.
Propositions can express nothing of what is higher. (6.42)

It is clear that ethics cannot be put into words.
Ethics is transcendental.
(Ethics and aesthetics are one and the same.) (6.421)

And finally,

God does not reveal himself *in* the world. (6.432)

Thus, the logical and pictorial form of language (its sense), the metaphysical subject, the sense of the world itself, all value, and God lie outside the world. To view the world as a limited whole, then, means to view it *apart* from, as excluding all these. And such a viewing (*Anschauung*) is what Wittgenstein calls the *mystical.*

[5] Presumably, we should also have to say this of objects (*Gegenstände*), though Wittgenstein does not speak of them in this context. But it is difficult to decide what his views are about this, since he "defines" facts (*Sachverhalte*) as *combinations* of objects (2.01).

Feeling the world as a limited whole — it is this that is mystical. (6.45)

To view the world as a limited whole, to view it as finite, to view it mystically, all mean to view it *both* as the totality of facts *and* as radically excluding and contrasted with all that is *not* fact. The world as world, as mere fact, can be fully grasped only in contrast to what is not fact. And both these aspects must be viewed together in order for the radical finitude of the world and its mystical character to become manifest. Now, the facts being simply the *how* of the world, all that lies outside the world may be called its *existence* — *that* the world is. The mystical, then, is co-extensive with the *existence* of the world.

It is not *how* things are in the world that is mystical, but *that* it exists. (6.44)

What is mystical is *that* there is anything at all — *that* there are any facts — rather than nothing.

Finally, all that lies outside the world — the totality of the mystical — is everything that cannot be "put into words". This is obviously a corollary of the view that everything that can be put into words is limited to the realm of possible facts. Hence, all that is not fact is coextensive with all that cannot be spoken about or expressed (*gesagt*).

There are, indeed, things that cannot be put into words. They *make themselves manifest*. They are what is mystical. (6.522)

The logical form of language, the sense of the world, solipsism, value and God are the mystical because they cannot be put into words but only make themselves manifest.

(C). Many philosophers have attempted to speak about such matters, that is, they have attempted to "put into words" questions about the nature of value, the meaning of life, the existence and nature of God, etc. But for Wittgenstein a question that cannot be asked, a question regarding what cannot be spoken about, is not a genuine question. It is nonsensical (*unsinnig*).

For doubt can exist only where a question exists, a question only where an answer exists, and an answer only where something *can be said*. (6.51)

Everything that can be thought at all can be thought clearly. Everything that can be put into words can be put clearly. (4.116)

But,

What *can* be shown, *cannot* be said. (4.1212)

Since logical and pictorial form are the essence of language — the necessary and sufficient condition for its possibility — any language presupposes it. Thus, any attempt to *use* language to *say* what the logical form of language is is therefore an attempt to use language while at the same time transcending it. In short, it is an attempt to say what cannot be said. And such an "attempt" is self-contradictory and nonsensical.

But has not Wittgenstein himself tried to do just this in the *Tractatus*? That is, has not Wittgenstein tried to "say" what the logical form of language is, while at the same time denying the possibility of this attempt? And in doing so has he not contradicted himself? Are not the "propositions" of the *Tractatus* themselves nonsensical? Wittgenstein gives an affirmative answer to these questions, and indeed the affirmation of the self-contradictory, nonsensical character of the *Tractatus* in his last "word".

The correct method in philosophy would really be the following: to say nothing except what can be said, i.e., propositions of natural science — i.e. something that has nothing to do with philosophy... . (6.53)

My propositions serve as elucidations in the following way: anyone who understands me eventually recognizes them as nonsensical.... (6.54)

At this point we reach the final conclusion of Wittgenstein's whole thought, a conclusion, however, which has been implicit from the very beginning, and which has continually guided and formed it. This final conclusion is simply that the mystical — what cannot be said — *is philosophy itself.* Indeed, all the aspects of the mystical listed above are what have been traditionally conceived to be the "subject-matter" or "problems" of philosophy. It is philosophy itself, then, that is nonsensical. The real import of Wittgenstein's earlier assertions that philosophy is an activity, that it is not a doctrine, that there are no philosophical propositions

(4.112), is now clear. Philosophy is nonsensical because it does not state facts, and the range of possible facts is co-extensive with the range of what can be thought and meaningfully expressed. Instead, philosophy "sets the limit to what can be thought", and hence to what can be said (4.114-5).

But the limits of thought and expression cannot themselves be thought or expressed, for this presupposes transcending those limits, i.e., thinking the unthinkable and saying the unsayable. All philosophy can do is *show* (*zeigen*) those limits from "within" (4.115). Propositions which picture facts, the propositions of natural science, and the range of significant language coincide. And since philosophy does not picture facts, it is not one of the natural sciences (4.111), it transcends the limits of significant language. Nothing that is philosophical can be expressed. In this sense, philosophy is not even a *possibility*. Not only can it not answer the "questions" it seeks to answer but it cannot even *ask* them. Moreover, philosophy cannot even say this, i.e., philosophy cannot even say *that* such "questions" cannot be asked. Wittgenstein is committed not only to the paradox that philosophy is not a possibility, but he is also committed to holding — and he himself may not have fully grasped this — that the *denial* of this possibility is not a possibility.

The *Tractatus*, as an attempt to negate the possibility of philosophy transcends the limits of possible sense — it cannot be put into words, it is the mystical. But Wittgenstein tries to achieve this by *using* philosophy, that is, by trying to *say* that it is not possible. And on the basis of his own views one cannot say this. If philosophy is not a possibility one cannot say that philosophy is not a possibility, since this very saying is *itself* philosophical and hence presupposes that philosophy *is* a possibility. Wittgenstein at times seems aware of this, for he speaks of the only "correct method" of philosophy as the not saying of anything (philosophical) at all. All one can say are the propositions of natural science. Thus, if someone feels a temptation to "say" something philosophical we can only try to demonstrate (*nachweisen*) to him that what he is trying to say is nonsensical, i.e., cannot possibly be said. The correct method of philosophy is thus not a method *in* philosophy (6.53). It consists of simply enumerating the propositions of natural science, hoping that these particular "specimens" of sense will *show* that whatever does not conform to their general structure will be *non*-sensical. On the other hand, Wittgenstein himself does not adhere to his own prescription, since he wrote a philosophical book which ostensively attempts to "say" (for instance) what the proper method of philosophy is. And trying to "say" what the correct method of philosophy is is not the same thing as *applying* that method. However, aside from this, Wittgenstein seems quite willing to accept the force of his conclusions and apply them to his own case. Thus, he admits that the "propositions" in the *Tractatus* are nonsensical, and says that the fundamental lesson of his book is that the reader *recognize* (*erkennt*) this. If he does he will be enabled to transcend these pseudo-propositions. This is the meaning of the "ladder image".

> My propositions serve as elucidations in the following way: anyone who understands me eventually recognizes them as nonsensical, when he has used them — as steps — to climb up beyond them. (He must, so to speak, throw away the ladder after he has climbed up it.)
>
> He must transcend these propositions, and then he will see the world aright. (6.54)

It is not *through* philosophy that one "sees the world aright". One can see the world aright only when one has completely transcended philosophy, i.e., recognized the impossibility of its possibility. The *Tractatus*, then, negates itself. It negates itself because it is an attempt to negate the possibility of philosophy *in and through* philosophy itself. This is only another way of saying that it is an attempt to say what cannot be said.

Let me apply this same line of argument to the particular problems dealt with in this book. I said earlier that Wittgenstein has no "theory" of either meaning or truth. The reason I gave was simply that meaning and truth are not *facts*, and all genuine theories are about facts. In the context of the present criticism this point can be carried further. Wittgenstein has a view of meaning which, if "true" implies that the view itself is *without* meaning (*unsinnig*), since the sentences which state the view (e.g., the sentence: "What a picture represents is its sense" (2.221)) do not conform to the necessary and sufficient conditions for meaningful language stipulated in the view. This is just an implication of the claim that the logical form of language can only be *shown* — is mystical — and cannot be "put into words" (*gesagt*). But if the view is without meaning it cannot be true. Similarly, Wittgenstein has a view of truth which, if "true", would imply that the sentences expressing the view (e.g., the sentence: "The agreement or disagreement of its [a picture's] sense with reality constitutes its truth or falsity" (2.222)) could not themselves be true, for *they* do not represent states of affairs. There is a fundamental difference of logical type between the sentences which express a theory of truth and the sentences which (in being true) *conform* to the theory. Moreover, Wittgenstein has construed this difference of logical type so radically that, although all true propositions state facts, the statement *that* this is so is not itself a factual statement. Thus, Wittgenstein holds a view about truth which, by its very nature, makes it impossible to account for the "truth" of the view itself. Indeed, if the view is true it cannot be true.

The final outcome of the *Tractatus* is *nihilism*. This nihilism is not only the view that value and meaning lie "outside" the world, that any attempt to put them into words is nonsensical, although it is partly this. These forms of nihilism have been presented before, in one guise or another. They have been asserted by some philosophers and denied by others. The nihilism at the heart of the *Tractatus*, however, is deeper rooted and more profound. It is a nihilism which negates the very possibility of philosophy itself. And it is this negation that is the real meaning of the last pronouncement of the work, which, although it is last, it also its major thought.

What we cannot speak about we must consign to silence. (7)

In his Preface Wittgenstein says that the *Tractatus* deals with the problems of philosophy, and shows that these problems arise out of a misunderstanding of the logic of language.[6] Philosophy, then, is essentially the "critique of language", which critique aims at showing that all philosophical propositions are nonsensical. Philosophy has achieved its goal when this is recognized, i.e., when the "problems" of philosophy are seen to be pseudo-problems. In this sense they are "solved", or more exactly, *dis*-solved.

> On the other hand the *truth* of the thoughts that are here set forth seems to me unassailable and definitive. I therefore believe myself to have found, on all essential points, the final solution of the problems.[7]

However, as we have seen, this "truth" cannot be expressed. Even the attempt to *show* it is impossible, since such showing either takes the form of a "speaking" (e.g., the writing of the sentences of the *Tractatus)* which is nonsensical, or else retreats to the position that nothing philosophical can be even uttered (e.g., enumerating the propositions of natural science). But *these* are themselves philosophical views and thus nonsensical and not possible. Wittgenstein did not fully realize the ultimate implication of his whole thought, namely, that *not only is the Tractatus* (by his own admission) *nonsensical, but his attempt to show this is itself nonsensical.*

I have argued in these final pages that Wittgenstein's attempt to negate the possibility of philosophy is a failure. It is a failure because such a negation is itself an impossibility. On the basis of this I believe that perhaps the most valuable contribution of the *Tractatus* lies in the fact that, in being one of the most serious and profound attempts to destroy philosophy, it illustrates all the more clearly and forcefully that this cannot be done. Its most serious shortcoming, then, is that it is a "philosophy" which cannot account for the possibility of itself. Thus, the "self-refuting" character of the *Tractatus,* which Wittgenstein himself explicitly alludes to at the end of his work (6.54), is not *merely* that the propositions contained in it are nonsensical. Rather, it is that even *this* cannot be *shown,* for to do so presupposes that philosophy is possible, which possibility is precisely what has been denied. I

[6] *Tractatus,* p. 3.
[7] *Ibid.*, p. 5.

conclude that no attempt to negate the possibility of philosophy can succeed, and that a necessary condition for an adequate philosophy is that it be able to account for its own possibility.

But, as Hegel once pointed out, the surest and most direct, indeed the only means of demonstrating the possibility of philosophy is for philosophy to demonstrate itself as an *actuality*. Perhaps this will be not entirely forgotten, and the study of the *Tractatus* may have as one of its fruits the reawakening of the meaning of the question of philosophy and of its genuine possibility.

SELECTED BIBLIOGRAPHY

Anscombe, G. E. M., *An Introduction to Wittgenstein's Tractatus* (London Hutchinson University Library, 1959).

——, "Mr. Copi on Objects, Properties and Relations in the *Tractatus*", *Mind,* LXVIII, No, 271 (July 1959), p. 404.

Bernstein, Richard, "Wittgenstein's Three Languages", *Review of Metaphysics,* XV, No. 2 (December 1961), pp. 278-298.

Black, Max, *Language and Philosophy* (Ithaca, New York, Cornell University Press, 1949).

——, *The Nature of Mathematics* (Paterson, New Jersey, Littlefield, Adams & Co., 1959).

——, *Philosophical Analysis: A Collection of Essays* (Ithaca, New York, Cornell University Press, 1950.)

Carnap, Rudolf, *The Logical Syntax of Language* (New York, Harcourt, Brace and Company, 1937).

Copi, I. M., "Objects, Properties and Relations in the *Tractatus*", *Mind,* LXVII, No. 266 (April 1958), pp. 145-165.

——, Review of Stenius' *Wittgenstein's Tractatus: A Critical Exposition,* in *Philosophical Review,* LXXII, No. 3, pp. 382-390.

Cornford, F. M., *Plato's Theory of Knowledge* (New York, Library of Liberal Arts Press, 1957).

Daitz, Edna, "The Picture Theory of Meaning", *Essays in Conceptual Analysis,* ed. by Anthony Flew (London, MacMillan & Co. Ltd., 1960).

Demos, Raphael, "A Discussion of a Certain Type of Negative Proposition", *Mind,* XXVI, No. 101 (January 1917), pp. 188-196.

Evans, Ellis, "About 'aRb'", *Mind,* LXVIII, No. 272 (October 1959), pp. 535-538.

——, "*Tractatus* 3.1432", *Mind,* LXIV, No. 254 (April 1955), pp. 259-260.

Frege, Gottlob, *Translations from the Philosophical Writings of Gottlob Frege,* ed. by P. Geach and M. Black (Oxford, Basil Blackwell, 1960).

Geach, P. T., "Review of the *Tractatus-Logico-Philosophicus* in the Italian translation by Gian Carlo Colombo", *Philosophical Review,* LXVI, No. 4 (October 1957), pp. 556-559.

Harrison, Frank R., "Notes on Wittgenstein's Use of '*das Mystische*'", *The Southern Journal of Philosophy,* I, No. 3 (Fall 1963), pp. 3-9.

Hawkins, D. J. B., "Wittgenstein and the Cult of Language", *Crucial Problems of Modern Philosophy* (University of Notre Dame Press, 1962).

Hintikka, Jaakko. "On Wittgenstein's 'Solipsism'", *Mind,* LXVII, No. 265 (January 1958), pp. 88-91.

Hume, David, *A Treatise of Human Nature*, Vol. I (New York, E. P. Dutton & Co., 1961).

Kant, Immanuel, *Critique of Pure Reason*, 2nd ed., trans. by N. K. Smith (London, MacMillan & Co. Ltd., 1961).

Malcolm, Norman, *Ludwig Wittgenstein, A Memoir* (London, Oxford University Press, 1958).

Maslow, Alexander P., *A Study of Ludwig Wittgenstein's Tractatus Logico-Philosophicus* (Berkeley, Cal., University of California Press, 1961).

Moore, Willis, "Structure in Sentence and in Fact", *Philosophy of Science*, V, No. 1 (January 1938), pp. 81-88.

O'Brien, G. D., *Meaning and Fact: A Study in the Philosophy of Wittgenstein*, unpublished doctoral dissertation, University of Chicago, 1960.

Paul, G. A. "Wittgenstein", in *The Revolution in Philosophy* (London, MacMillan & Co. Ltd., 1960).

Peirce, C. S., *Collected Papers*, Vol. IV (Cambridge, Mass., Harvard University Press, 1933).

Plato, *The Dialogues of Plato*, 2 Vols., trans. by B. Jowett (New York, Random House, 1937).

Plochmann, G. K., Review of G. E. M. Anscombe's *An Introduction to Wittgenstein's Tractatus*, *The Modern Schoolman*, XXXVII, No. 3 (March 1960), pp. 242-246.

——, and J. B. Lawson, *Terms in Their Propositional Contexts in Wittgenstein's Tractatus: An Index* (Illinois, So. Illinois University Press, 1962).

Ramsey, F. P., *The Foundations of Mathematics* (Paterson, New Jersey, Littlefield, Adams & Co., 1960).

Rhees, R., "Miss Anscombe on the *Tractatus*", *The Philosophical Quarterly*, X, No. 38 (January 1960), pp. 21-31.

Russell, Bertrand, *Logic and Knowledge* (London, Georg Allen & Unwin Ltd., 1956).

——, & Whitehead, Alfred North, *Principia Mathematica to *56*, 2nd ed. (Cambridge, University Press, 1962).

Ryle, Gilbert., "Ludwig Wittgenstein", *Analysis*, XII, No. 1 (October 1951), pp. 1-9.

Schopenhauer, Arthur, *The World as Will and Representation*, 2 Vols., trans. by E. F. J. Payne (Indian Hills, Colorado, Falcon's Wing Press, 1958).

Stenius, Erik, *Wittgenstein's Tractatus: A Critical Exposition of its Main Lines of Thought* (Oxford, Basil Blackwell, 1960).

Strawson, P. F., "On Referring", *Essays in Conceptual Analysis*, ed. by Antony Flew, (London, MacMillan & Co. Ltd., 1960).

Urmson, J. O., *Philosophical Analysis* (Oxford, Clarendon Press, 1956).

Warnock, G. J., *English Philosophy Since 1900* (London, Oxford University Press, 1958).

Weinberg, Julius R., *An Examination of Logical Positivism* (Paterson, New Jersey, Littlefield, Adams & Co., 1960).

Wittgenstein, Ludwig, *Notebooks 1914-1916*, ed. by G. E. M. Anscombe and G. H. von Wright (Oxford, Basil Blackwell, 1961).

——, *Philosophical Investigations*, trans. by G. E. M. Anscombe (New York, MacMillan Co., 1953).

Wittgenstein, Ludwig, "Some Remarks on Logical Form", *Proceedings of the Aristotelian Society*, Supplement, IX (1929), pp. 162-71.

——, *Tractatus Logico-Philosophicus*, trans. by C. K. Ogden (London, Routledge & Kegan Paul Ltd., 1922. Eighth imp., 1960).

——, *Tractatus Logico-Philosophicus*, trans. by D. F. Pears and B. F. McGuinness (London, Routledge & Kegan Paul, 1961).